D0454978

"Here's a book that sticks to the very basics of the message of our Lord Jesus Christ. I have known Peter for almost half a century and seen this message – that we need to find our identity in Christ alone – worked out in his life. I pray you will not just read it but give copies to others. Relevant, important, and biblical, it is urgently needed in the confusing and complex days in which we live. This has been the most important message in my life."

George Verwer, founder of Operation Mobilisation

"In our culture, issues of personal identity and security are now the hot topics of pressing concern in a confused and unstable world. Drawing on a lifetime experience of Christian service and global leadership, Peter Maiden tackles these fundamental themes with his characteristic honesty, biblical clarity and practical wisdom. Very counter-cultural, challenging and encouraging!"

Jonathan Lamb, minister-at-large, Keswick Ministries

"An important book on a crucial theme from a deeply respected servant of the Lord. Peter Maiden draws on his wide experience to explore the liberating truth of who we are in Christ, as believers. His insights are important for all Christians and especially challenging for leaders."

John Risbridger, chair, Keswick Ministries

"Contemporary culture has left many of us feeling unwanted, unloved and incompetent. If we find our identity in the passing opinions of our age then, eventually, we are likely to feel worthless. In this magnificent book, Peter Maiden gives us a whole fresh perspective on our identity. With a blend of the

wisdom of experience and an extensive knowledge of scripture, he demonstrates our real worth and purpose in our identity in Christ. Brimming with encouragement, but laced with challenge, this is a book to transform lives."

Chris Sinkinson, Moorlands Bible College

"Finding identity in Christ sounds great, but what does it actually mean? Building on the Rock *offers down-to-earth answers. Peter Maiden shows how the Bible fizzes with contemporary relevance. But better than that, he shows how its message is truly liberating in our performance-obsessed culture."*

Tim Chester, author of over 30 books.

"I need ongoing, practical encouragement in keeping looking to Jesus, and to keep on finding my identity and sense of worth in Him. And I know I'm not alone in this. Peter Maiden brings that encouragement to many, myself included. It's a delight to read this book, to walk alongside Peter, and to be pointed to Jesus. Whether you're new to the Christian faith, wondering if it's worth your attention, or a seasoned follower of Jesus, this book will warm and help you. Peter writes from a life-long journey of following Jesus, and finding his own identity in what Jesus has done. Here is a book shaped by years of living out of the promises of Scripture, in different places and in every kind of circumstance. It is a book which lifts my eyes from myself to a wonderful Lord, and which will do the same for you. I hope you cherish that prospect."

Matthew Sleeman, Oakhill College

Building on the Rock

FINDING YOUR IDENTITY IN CHRIST

Peter Maiden

MONARCH
BOOKS

Oxford UK, and Grand Rapids, USA

Published by Monarch Books
an imprint of
Lion Hudson plc
Wilkinson House, Jordan Hill Road,
Oxford OX2 8DR, England
Email: monarch@lionhudson.com
www.lionhudson.com/monarch

ISBN 978-0-85721-759-2
e-ISBN 978-0-85721-760-8

First edition 2016

Acknowledgments
Unless otherwise mentioned, Scripture quotations are taken from the Holy Bible, New International Version Anglicised. Copyright © 1979, 1984, 2011 Biblica, formerly International Bible Society. Used by permission of Hodder & Stoughton Ltd, an Hachette UK company. All rights reserved. "NIV" is a registered trademark of Biblica. UK trademark number 1448790.
Scripture quotations marked AV or KJV are from The Authorized (King James) Version. Rights in the Authorized Version are vested in the Crown. Reproduced by permission of the Crown's patentee, Cambridge University Press.
Scripture quotations marked ESV are from The Holy Bible, English Standard Version® (ESV®) copyright © 2001 by Crossway, a publishing ministry of Good News Publishers. All rights reserved.
Scripture quotations marked NASB are from the New American Standard Bible®, Copyright © 1960, 1962, 1963, 1968, 1971, 1972, 1973, 1975, 1977, 1995 by The Lockman Foundation. Used by permission.
Scripture quotations marked The Message are from The Message. Copyright © by Eugene H. Peterson 1993, 1994, 1995, 1996, 2000, 2001, 2002. Used by permission of NavPress Publishing Group.

A catalogue record for this book is available from the British Library

Printed and bound in the UK, June 2016, LH26

Dedication

To Dan and Becks and the climb up Carrick Fell.

Contents

Acknowledgments

Thank you to Ali Hull, Commissioning Editor for Lion Hudson. She encouraged me to write the book, assured me when I was losing heart, and persisted with me to completion. Thanks, Ali! Thanks to my friend, Reverend Dr Matthew Sleeman of Oakhill College, and to copy-editor Drew Stanley: they both helped me greatly with their feedback.

CHAPTER ONE

Who Do You Think You Are?

Am I the sum of the things that I do? This was a rather urgent question for me as my sixty-fifth birthday drew near. I was the International Director of Operation Mobilisation. I had been chairman of the Keswick Convention. I had been co-chairman of the board of a Bible college, and on the board of a number of other Christian organizations. I had decided that I should stand down from all of these responsibilities by the time of my sixty-fifth birthday. Was there life without these positions? Did they make up my identity? Or was I gradually giving my identity away, role by role?

One of the organizations I was associated with held an annual get-together. As we arrived we all received the usual name tag. One year the designation on my tag was "Chairman", the next year it was "Trustee". And the year after that, it read "Attendee". Was my life ebbing away?

Not quite. There was still my physical exercise. Approaching sixty-five, I was still running regularly, cycling, and working out at the gym. Runners love to tell the stories of their achievements, and their injuries! And the knees after a lifetime of running had begun to cry out for mercy. Would this soon be a thing of the past? One thing was surely secure. I was a husband, father of three, and grandfather of nine, and my family roles and responsibilities played a huge and wonderful part in my life.

Identity definers

Who are you? Are you the sum of the things you do? Is your life defined by your achievements? What if you can no longer do the things you used to? I have indicated some of the areas in my life which could so easily have defined my identity, and sadly sometimes did. There are so many others.

Your physical appearance can become your identity definer. If you were asked "Who are you?", while you might not say "I am a handsome man" or "a beautiful woman", that is what might matter most to you. Or it might be that you want to appear younger than you are – so that people think "She's only forty" when in fact she is over fifty. Huge amounts are spent on cosmetic surgeries, sometimes even on procedures that can threaten our long-term health. But still a quarter of all Brits admit to not feeling good about their looks.

What about the sportsperson who has had a goal to which everything must play second fiddle? I am thinking as I write of someone who was getting towards what we might call midlife, when he got into a demanding sport. I watched with real sadness as it gradually took him over. He wasn't happy in his job and his marriage wasn't strong, so improving his personal best in his chosen discipline became his identity definer, and quite obviously the basis of his self-worth.

For many people, the most important identity definer in their lives is their job, and the status it brings. I have known business and professional people for whom work, the growing of their business, or their career has been their identity definer. Marriages have come under severe strain, and even failed; children have felt as though they had no parents, certainly no parents who considered them to be a priority. An organization has been formed in the City of London called City Fathers. City Mothers has been going for some time and boasts over 3,000 members. The mastermind behind the two organizations says there is a great need to change the culture of the City. It is a culture where long working hours are the norm and the expected. I read of one couple where the father is an employment lawyer working up to sixty hours a week, attempting to juggle the care of his two young children with his wife, who is also a lawyer. Both of the children are in nursery from 7:30 a.m. to 6 p.m. each day and a member of the nursery staff drives them home at the end of their day. Nearly half of 753 fathers surveyed by the organization described "missing their children" as their biggest daily challenge. Some 45 per cent described their work–life balance as less than satisfactory.

For many of us, being in a relationship is crucial if we are to feel we have any worth. If nobody wants to ask us out, we must be nobodies. When we are in a relationship, if it's going well, our self-worth is bolstered, but if it's going through rough times, it will not be long before the nagging questions are heard again: Am I really needed? Am I really attractive? Even in marriage, we can want constant reassurance that our partner still loves us.

One of the reasons for the popularity of dating apps is that you can see someone you fancy and avoid the rejection that potentially follows asking them out. You simply send them a virtual wink on your phone. The Tinder app presents you with a huge number of potential partners. If you like them, you simply "swipe right". If they like you they can respond and you become a match. But if they don't, you hear nothing, you remain unaware anyone ever "swiped left", and at least your ego is unaffected.

In our consumer culture the people who can "splash the cash" are admired, and a person's worth to some degree at least is seen in their ability to purchase. So our possessions can become a way of identifying ourselves, particularly before others – from the car we drive to the watch we wear. It may be very important to us that others know where we spend our holidays or which school our children go to. Or that our suits come from Armani and our shoes from Jimmy Choo. Advertisers play on these fears and wishes at every turn.

For some, family is absolutely everything, and our self-worth can be dependent on our children. We live to experience their affection or to glory in their success. Some parents are so keen that their children should do well, they start them studying as soon as they can, or fill up their time with so many activities that, as teenagers, the children risk burnout.

Volunteering can become an identity definer. I have come across those who may not find much self-worth in other areas of their lives, and so volunteer to work with an organization. Their apparent self-sacrifice in doing this, and the appreciation they are shown for what they do, become the source of their self-worth. Helping others is another common identity definer. Timothy Keller writes: "Often one person in a relationship is needy and constantly in trouble, and the other person is the counsellor-rescuer. How the needy person uses the rescuer is obvious. What is less obvious is that the rescuer is using the needy person as well. He or she needs them to get a sense of worth and/or a sense of moral superiority. He/she needs to be needed."[1]

I know only too well that Christian ministry for some of us can meet our need for self-worth. I have often had to ask myself, "Who am I serving God for? Is this really for God, for His glory, or is it more about me? Am I more interested in the satisfaction, the status, and the appreciation I receive from others for what I do?"

The list of identity definers could continue for many paragraphs.

> Glynn Harrison explains the different advice which would be offered today to someone complaining of feeling a little bit low compared to fifty years ago.
>
> "Fifty years ago the advice would be; Don't get stuck in your own problems. Don't think about yourself so much. Instead of being a 'here am I' sort of person,

1 Timothy Keller, *Judges for You*, The Good Book Company, 2013, page 155.

try to be a 'there you are person.' Think about other people. Try to get out more. Make new friends and explore some new interests."

But today the advice would be:

"You need to believe in yourself more! Stop thinking so much about other people's problems and worrying about other people's expectations. You need to discover who you are. Be yourself. Learn to like yourself. Build up your self-esteem."[2]

Building on sand

What is common to all of the identity definers mentioned above is their uncertainty. What if the person whose identity is in their physical appearance is disfigured? We have all seen the desperate attempts to iron out the wrinkles and flatten out the bulges as the years pass. What if the sportsperson is injured, and can no longer perform? Simon Barnes made some perceptive comments in *The Times* (21 April 2014) about the cricketer Jonathan Trott, a gifted batsman who played some great innings for England. He had to return from the Ashes tour of Australia because of stress-related illness. After attempting to start his career again he sadly had to withdraw from all cricket. This is what Simon wrote; "It's not that he is unable to take part in an amusing or stimulating pastime. Playing cricket is Trott's function in life; batting is not his pastime, but his meaning. It's more than being unable to do his job. Trott has lost his place in the world. He defined

2 Glynn Harrison, *The Big Ego Trip*, Downers Grove, IL: Inter-Varsity Press, 2013, pages 15 and 16.

himself by what he did on the cricket field, and now he can't do it. Perhaps not at all, perhaps not ever. He was once exceptional. He is now in cricketing terms, nothing. He has lost more than his job; he has lost himself."

What if the children move to another part of the world, or for some reason turn against you? You must have witnessed the tragedy of parents relying on the achievements of their children as their identity definer. Totally unreasonable expectations are placed on them, so easily causing emotional damage. How many children have struggled because they felt they could never quite come up to their parents' expectations? And even marriages fail, or partners die.

In the recent recession, we have seen so many businesses, built with huge commitment over the years, going belly-up. I can think of a young man who took over the family business, rapidly building it up. He was being feted as a business genius. Then he tried one merger too many when the banks were lending as if there was no tomorrow. The financial situation changed and the bank lenders, who had seemed so flexible and generous, appeared to change character overnight. He had the enormous shock and shame of the administrators entering the headquarters of his business, and giving him thirty minutes to collect his personal effects from the office and leave.

The argument of this book is that our lives, our identity, and our sense of worth must be based on a surer foundation. It must be based on a foundation that the storms of life, however intensely they rage, cannot destroy. I write with the absolute conviction that there is such a foundation.

Read Daniel 2.

This was a man who surely had everything going for him. If ever a man should have considered himself a success, it is Nebuchadnezzar at this point. Everything is going his way. He is only in the second year of his reign, and already it has been immensely successful. He has defeated the Egyptians, moved on into Syria and Palestine, laid siege to Jerusalem, and the Israelites, including Daniel, are now under his control. Everyone knows who he is. His identity is clear, he is the king, and the extent of his rule is enormous.

Daniel says to him, "Your Majesty, you are the king of kings. The God of heaven has given you dominion and power and might and glory; in your hands he has placed all mankind and the beasts of the field and the birds in the sky. Wherever they live, he has made you ruler over them all" (Daniel 2:37–38). Nebuchadnezzar must be thinking, "It doesn't get better than this." But this immensely powerful man has a problem. He can't sleep. "As Your Majesty was lying there, your mind turned to things to come" (Daniel 2:29). Dreams trouble him, ruining what should have been the enjoyment of all his privilege and power. "I have all this stuff, but how long can I possibly keep it?" he wonders. "It could be torn from me as quickly as I received it." He is desperate to hear the interpretation of his dream. He will go to the cruellest extremes, and offer the most fantastic rewards, if only he can know the future (Daniel 2:5–6).

Read again of the dream that so troubled the king. Then look at the interpretation of the dream which God gave through Daniel. It is a dream which describes four great human kingdoms (verses 39–40). The kingdoms or empires being described were most probably the Babylonian, Medo-Persian, Greek, and Roman ones. But there is a fifth kingdom, depicted by the rock cut out of the mountain (verses 44–45): this is the kingdom of King Jesus. You will see that nothing can stand before the growth of this kingdom. Those kingdoms which at times appear so stable and permanent eventually collapse and disappear, while this kingdom triumphs. It is so vital to have the foundation of your life and your identity based not on human position, power, and privilege, but on Christ the King and His eternal kingdom.

CHAPTER TWO

Start from the Right Place

Read Philippians 3:1–14:

Further, my brothers and sisters, rejoice in the Lord! It is no trouble for me to write the same things to you again, and it is a safeguard for you. Watch out for those dogs, those evildoers, those mutilators of the flesh. For it is we who are the circumcision, we who serve God by his Spirit, who boast in Christ Jesus, and who put no confidence in the flesh – though I myself have reasons for such confidence.

If someone else thinks they have reasons to put confidence in the flesh, I have more: circumcised on the eighth day, of the people of Israel, of the tribe of Benjamin, a Hebrew of Hebrews; in regard to the law, a Pharisee; as for zeal, persecuting the church; as for righteousness based on the law, faultless.

But whatever were gains to me I now consider loss for the sake of Christ. What is more, I consider everything a loss because of the surpassing worth of knowing Christ Jesus my Lord, for whose sake I have lost all things. I consider them garbage, that I may gain Christ and be found in him, not having a righteousness of my own that comes from the law, but that which is through faith in Christ – the righteousness that comes from God on the basis of faith. I want to know Christ – yes, to know the power of his resurrection and participation in his sufferings, becoming like him in his death, and so, somehow, attaining to the resurrection from the dead.

Not that I have already obtained all this, or have already arrived at my goal, but I press on to take hold of that for which Christ Jesus took hold of me. Brothers and sisters, I do not consider myself yet to have taken hold of it. But one thing I do: Forgetting what is behind and straining towards what is ahead, I press on towards the goal to win the prize for which God has called me heavenward in Christ Jesus.

Once when asking directions to a city, to my surprise the person responded by saying, "Where have you come from?" His question didn't seem relevant but starting from the right place is vital.

Is life all about me, my work, and my achievements? If we are going to understand who we are, indeed if we are going to understand life, we must begin with God, not ourselves. Why did God create us? What did He want His creation to be? What did He want us to do?

Successful failure!

It is frighteningly possible that we could achieve great things, even fulfil all our goals in life, and yet never understand who God made us to be, and why we are here on this planet. We could be a stunning success in the eyes of the majority, but find that, on God's examination, we have wasted our lives. A famous author, Jack Higgins, was asked, "What do you wish you had been told when you were a child that no one actually told you?" He replied, "I wish someone had explained that when you finally make it to the top there is nothing there." Augustine wrote, "Our hearts are restless until they find their rest in thee." Deep down we know we were created for something far bigger than anything this "me" culture is offering as prizes.

The apostle Paul had great privileges and achieved outstanding things. This is how he describes his early life, "circumcised on the eighth day, of the people of Israel, of the tribe of Benjamin, a Hebrew of Hebrews; in regard to the law, a Pharisee; as for zeal, persecuting the church; as for righteousness based on the law, faultless" (Philippians 3:5–6). These were Saul's, as he then was, identity definers. I am sure he walked around with his head held high. He was from the right stock, and his parents had given him a good start. He grew up a man of conviction, "persecuting the church", and devotion: "as for righteousness, based on the law, faultless".

Actually the word "devotion" is totally inadequate. When you realize the multitude of laws a Jew had to keep each day, to say that in that regard he was faultless is an incredible statement. This was a man of extreme devotion. His parents must have been utterly delighted, and totally proud of him. He certainly made the most of the good start they had given him. But one day he realized it was all garbage (verse 8). Paul could look back to a day, in fact a specific moment in time, and in his case even a specific place, when and where he knew he had got it all wrong. He had been living life with great energy and conviction, and probably receiving many accolades for doing so, but he knew in a moment that all his achievements were worthless because his life had been built on the kind of uncertain foundation we mentioned in the first chapter.

Paul seems to use the language of accountancy. He thought he had been building up a significant amount of profit, but he found himself in loss from which he could not recover without divine intervention. At this point the great reversal took place in Paul's theological convictions: from "confidence in the flesh" (verse 4) to "faith in Christ" (verse 8). From self (verses 4–6) to God (verses 7–11). From being "the finished article" (verses 4–6) to pressing on (verses 12–14). Paul encourages the Philippians to "put no confidence in the flesh" (verse 3) because he had learned that, if you do, your confidence will be built on a shaky human foundation, and it will be just a matter of time before it collapses.

This great reversal went hand in hand with a great exchange. When Paul turned from "confidence in the flesh" to "faith in Christ", God took his sins away at the cross, and clothed him with the righteousness of Jesus. Paul exchanged the dirty rags of his own life for a spotless robe. Now Paul knew that he was wholly accepted by God, not because he was righteous, but because God's own righteous Son had died in his place and was raised from death. Paul later explained this great exchange: "God made him who had no sin to be sin for us, so that in him we might become the righteousness of God" (2 Corinthians 5:21).

It's impossible to escape the strength of Paul's language here. Either we can have confidence in the flesh, or we can have faith in Christ. It is not as though there is a double foundation and you can have a foot on both. You rely either on your own achievements, or on Christ's achievement for you at the cross. The words of the old hymn "Rock of Ages" sum it up perfectly:

Nothing in my hand I bring
Simply to thy cross I cling.
Naked, come to Thee for dress,
Helpless look to Thee for grace.
Foul, I to the fountain fly.
Wash me, Saviour, or I die.

Augustus Toplady

Any other foundation will turn out to be a house built on sand.

The supreme permanent identity definer

Paul had come to boast in just one thing. A Person, and a relationship with that Person, had become the totally solid foundation of his life. Jesus had become his identity definer. He knew that in Christ he had been brought into a personal relationship with God. God had become his Father; his identity now was "child of God" because of Christ, not on his own merits. It's impossible to beat that. The professional titles I mentioned at the beginning of this book pale into absolute insignificance compared with this. As mentioned, all of those titles must be either freely given up or taken away, but this is permanent, it's an eternal reality. It is not dependent on my continuing performance. There will be no annual appraisal to see how I have performed. There will be no review with the question, "Should he continue in this position?" Time doesn't change it, sin won't destroy it, and Satan can't steal it.

I wrote earlier that I am convinced that there is an identity definer that none of the storms of life can steal from us. This is it! Who am I? Am I the sum of the things that I do? No. In fact, my true identity is determined not by something that I *do*, but by something that has been *done* for me. Paul had discovered and experienced "a righteousness that comes from God on the basis of faith" (Philippians 3:9). But are we going to trust and rely on Christ alone and completely? Do we understand His majesty sufficiently to do so? Do we understand how complete and perfect was the work that He did at the cross? Or do we still feel we need to make our contribution, a little bit of "do it yourself" righteousness?

Paul's standing before God, and his self-understanding, were not now based on his efforts, as they had previously been, but on the perfect work of another, the Lord Jesus. Because Paul had met the risen Jesus on the road to Damascus, h knew that what Jesus did on the cross had atoned for his sin before his Father. He knew that God had raised Jesus from the dead, expressing His complete satisfaction with what Jesus had done.

Paul was now so bound up with Christ, rather than himself, that the two words "in Christ" became fundamental to his writings. He knew that he was righteous in Christ, complete in Christ, fully alive in Christ, absolutely new in Christ, totally accepted in Christ, and absolutely secure. Paul was a man in Christ.

Not only does Paul describe himself as being "in Christ", he also writes that Christ lives in him. "It is no longer I who live, but Christ who lives in me. And the life I now live in the flesh I live by faith in the Son of God, who loved me and gave himself for me" (Galatians 2:20, ESV). It would take many pages to expound this wonderful personal testimony from Paul, but one thing is clear: His life is no longer ego-centred, concentrated on his achievements. Instead, it is totally Christ-centred. The identity definers for Paul have been totally transformed.

I am a child of God. I have been adopted into the family of the living God. I have a Father who loves me. It is covenant love. God has promised to love me, and that promise is unconditional. It is not based on my performance. You may fall out with someone, and be so disappointed that if they come back to you looking for the relationship to be restored, you would respond, "You have done nothing to earn it." It is exactly the case in our relationship with God, and He could justifiably respond in the same way. But

He doesn't. We do not have to earn His love. He has freely, unconditionally, chosen to love us. If you ask, "Why?", then the only answer is, "Because He is love."

This is the very core of our identity. By the grace of God, and the work of Christ, we are children of God, made in His image, and now encouraged to use intimate family terminology when we address God. We are encouraged to call out, "Abba, Father."

> We must keep reminding ourselves what we have and are in Christ. One of the great purposes of daily Bible reading, meditation and prayer is... to remember who and what we are. We need to say to ourselves: "Once I was a slave, but God has made me his son and put the spirit of his son into my heart. How can I turn back to the old slavery?" Again: "Once I did not know God, but now I know him and have come to be known by him. How can I turn back to the old ignorance?"[3]

3 John Stott, *The Message of Galatians*, The Bible Speaks Today series, London and Downers Grove, IL: Inter-Varsity Press, 1968, page 110.

CHAPTER THREE

Who Do You Think You *Were*?

Read Luke 7:36–50:

> *When one of the Pharisees invited Jesus to have dinner with him, he went to the Pharisee's house and reclined at the table. A woman in that town who lived a sinful life learned that Jesus was eating at the Pharisee's house, so she came there with an alabaster jar of perfume. As she stood behind him at his feet weeping, she began to wet his feet with her tears. Then she wiped them with her hair, kissed them and poured perfume on them.*
>
> *When the Pharisee who had invited him saw this, he said to himself, "If this man were a prophet, he would know who is touching him and what kind of woman she is – that she is a sinner."*
>
> *Jesus answered him, "Simon, I have something to tell you."*
>
> *"Tell me, teacher," he said.*
>
> *"Two people owed money to a certain moneylender. One owed him five hundred denarii, and the other*

fifty. Neither of them had the money to pay him back, so he forgave the debts of both. Now which of them will love him more?"

Simon replied, "I suppose the one who had the bigger debt forgiven."

"You have judged correctly," Jesus said.

Then he turned towards the woman and said to Simon, "Do you see this woman? I came into your house. You did not give me any water for my feet, but she wet my feet with her tears and wiped them with her hair. You did not give me a kiss, but this woman, from the time I entered, has not stopped kissing my feet. You did not put oil on my head, but she has poured perfume on my feet. Therefore, I tell you, her many sins have been forgiven – as her great love has shown. But whoever has been forgiven little loves little."

Then Jesus said to her, "Your sins are forgiven."

The other guests began to say among themselves, "Who is this who even forgives sins?"

Jesus said to the woman, "Your faith has saved you; go in peace."

We cannot know *who* we are until we know *whose* we are.

Corey Haas was eight years old when he became the youngest person to receive a form of gene therapy. The result for him was that he went from using a white cane (because of sight problems) to being able to both ride a bike and play various sports. It is impossible to imagine what it must be like to go from physical darkness to light, from seeing nothing to seeing the grandeur of the mountains and the raging oceans, or the tiny fingers of a newborn child.

A meal with a difference

Simon is a Pharisee, quite a well-to-do one. He probably has money, and can afford a house built round an open courtyard. On a summer's evening, meals are eaten there, and, if a rabbi is at the meal, it is not unusual for all kinds of people to come into the courtyard to listen to his teaching. As they enter, there will be water available to pour over their dusty feet, as the roads of these days are little more than mud tracks.

Into the courtyard walks a woman of the street. It must be embarrassing for this Pharisee to have such a woman defiling his house. She stands behind Jesus, who is reclining on a couch at a low table. She is weeping, and her tears wet the feet of Jesus. She dries them with her hair, before pouring very costly perfume on them. Simon is indignant. "If this man were a prophet, he would know who is touching him and what kind of woman she is – that she is a sinner" (Luke 7:39).

As all this has been going on, there has been an embarrassed silence in the courtyard. Jesus breaks the silence. Jesus answered Simon (who had actually only spoken to himself): "Simon, I have something to tell you. Two men owed money to a certain moneylender. One owed him five hundred denarii, and the other fifty. Neither of them had the money to pay him back, so he cancelled the debts of both.

Now which of them will love him more?" Simon replied, "I suppose the one who had the bigger debt cancelled." "You have judged correctly," Jesus said (Luke 7:40–43).

I wonder how long it took for the penny to drop for Simon?

"Then he turned towards the woman and said to Simon, 'Do you see this woman? I came into your house. You did not give me any water for my feet, but she wet my feet with her tears and wiped them with her hair. You did not give me a kiss, but this woman, from the time I entered, has not stopped kissing my feet. You did not put oil on my head, but she has poured perfume on my feet. Therefore, I tell you, her many sins have been forgiven – for she loved much. But he who has been forgiven little loves little'" (Luke 7:44–47).

Jesus is not saying that what the woman did, or even her sacrificial love, has earned forgiveness. Her love is the fruit, showing that she has already experienced that forgiveness. This is confirmed at the end of the incident when Jesus says to her, "Your faith has saved you; go in peace" (verse 48). The message of the earlier parable – "they could not pay" (verse 42) – shows that the woman's new identity is a gift of grace, and Simon's only hope is for that same gift of grace.

The point of the story is that Simon didn't understand himself – and the unnamed woman did. Simon has no consciousness of need. He is absolutely sure his religious observances are all that God would require, and more. But the woman knows the reality of her heart, and that has driven her to seek salvation in Christ, and thus to have this overwhelming love for Him.

To truly know and understand who we are today, we must fully appreciate what we were yesterday.

An astonished apostle

Paul could never quite get over this. "For I am the least of the apostles and do not even deserve to be called an apostle, because I persecuted the church of God. But by the grace of God I am what I am" (1 Corinthians 15:9–10). "Even though I was once a blasphemer and a persecutor and a violent man, I was shown mercy because I acted in ignorance and unbelief. The grace of our Lord was poured out on me abundantly, along with the faith and love that are in Christ Jesus" (1 Timothy 1:13–14).

It seems that Paul carried this sense of shock, surprise, and wonder throughout his life. "When I think of what I was, how can I be what I am today?" As you can see from his writing, his one answer was grace. No wonder this became one of the great themes of his preaching and writing.

"'By the grace of God I am what I am.' It is certain that I am not what I ought to be. But, blessed be God, I am not what I once was." This was the testimony of the slave trader-cum-pastor and famous hymn writer, John Newton. In his diary Newton often referred to his shortcomings and failures, but he knew that he was "not what he once was". Again his explanation for this is grace, which prompted him to write those famous lines:

Amazing grace how sweet the sound
That saved a wretch like me.
I once was lost but now am found,
Was blind but now I see.

Forgetting and remembering

Paul chose to forget many things. He writes in Philippians 3:13 (ESV) of "forgetting what lies behind". This no doubt meant those things which locked him in the past. Perhaps they included bitterness about past wrongs he felt he had endured, even the memory of past sins which could so easily overwhelm him. But there were things that, rather than forgetting, he chose to constantly remember. We must do the same. We must never forget what we were before God's grace reached down to us. It is only as we remember how far we were away from God that we truly experience and enjoy the intimate relationship which is ours with God our Father today.

This is quite difficult for me. Born into a Christian home, learning the stories of Jesus on my mother's knee, I fell in love with Jesus as a young child. Although I have often not loved Jesus as I should, I cannot recall a day when I didn't love Him. This is a magnificent start in life, but it does have its problems. How does it feel to be far away from God, to have no personal relationship with Him? I cannot recall a day when I experienced that. I have to read the first few verses of Ephesians 2 from time to time to remind myself of what it means to be "without Christ".

You may not consider yourself either a slave trader, a prostitute, or a Pharisee, but there was a day when you were "dead in your sins" (Ephesians 2:1). It is true of all of us. We were "separated from the life of God" (Ephesians 4:18). That was because of our "transgressions and sins" (Ephesians 2:1) In other words, we rebelled against the way God wanted us to live, and fell far short of the standard God expected of us. Some did it very publicly, like the slave trader and the prostitute, others more privately, as we see in the Pharisee's smug pride of heart in Luke 7. In the story of the prodigal son, there are clearly two prodigals. One leaves home and blows it very obviously. He messes up big time; he knows it and others see it. The other stays at home and seems to do everything right, but his heart is crammed full of pride, bitterness, and self-serving.

That's what happens when you are "separated from the life of God", you live in your sins (Ephesians 2:2) and that means you follow "the ways of this world and of the ruler of the kingdom of the air, the spirit who is now at work in those who are disobedient". I know it is considered by some to be ridiculously out of date to believe in a personal devil, but Paul is saying when you are separated from the life of God you come under the devil's influence, and the influence of the values and standards of this age, which are in opposition to God and His kingdom. We were in bondage, "gratifying the cravings of our sinful nature and following its desires and thoughts" (Ephesians 2:3). The result of all this is that "we were by nature objects of wrath."

So before we trusted in Christ, we were dominated by the

secular culture of this age outside of us, and our sinful nature within us, both ruled by the devil. And because of that, we faced the wrath of God. It is not pleasant to think about these things but to truly understand, fully appreciate, and enjoy who we are today, we must understand who we *were*.

In 2 Peter 1:9, Peter writes of those who are short-sighted and blind, and have forgotten they have been cleansed from their former sins. What a sad state for a Christian to ever get into. As we reflect on who we were, and all that God has done in Christ to make us who we are now, love, devotion, and thanksgiving to our Saviour will result.

Made in the image of God, we bear the divine likeness. Human beings are amazing – we might even use that overused word, awesome! I still look up at the moon and think how incredible it is that we have the ingenuity to put a man on it. I don't think I understand the Large Hadron Collider machine in Switzerland and its 6.5 teraelectronvolts per beam, but it seems a pretty awesome achievement to me. And we all know that people are capable of such wonderful acts of kindness and sacrifice. As a runner, I am always moved when watching the London marathon with its thousands of ordinary people, who possibly a year before would never have dreamed of running one mile, never mind twenty-six. Then some noble cause motivates them and they are ready to train, five or six times a week, for months on end, pushing through the pain barrier again and again to make their contribution to the cause.

Yet human beings are also capable of staggering acts of cruelty and selfishness. It sometimes appears that human cruelty has reached a new level in recent days, but history would tell a different story. Just read Romans chapter one for starters! Made to rule the world, we are well on the way to ruining the world. We are glorious but broken; fallen and finished but for a God of grace and rescue.

> Philip Yancey in his beautiful book *What's So Amazing About Grace* writes that though with many words "their meaning rots away" over time, he keeps "circling back to grace", because it is the one grand theological word which has not been spoiled.
>
> "Many people 'say grace' before meals, acknowledging daily bread as a gift from God. We are *grateful* for someone's kindness, *gratified* by good news, *congratulated* when successful, *gracious* in hosting friends. When a person's service pleases us, we leave a *gratuity*. In each of these uses I hear a pang of childlike delight in the undeserved."[4]

4 Philip Yancey, *What's So Amazing About Grace*, Grand Rapids, MI: Zondervan, 1997, page 12.

CHAPTER FOUR

The Evangelical Slave

Read Galatians 2 and 4:4–7:

Then after fourteen years, I went up again to Jerusalem, this time with Barnabas. I took Titus along also. I went in response to a revelation and, meeting privately with those esteemed as leaders, I presented to them the gospel that I preach among the Gentiles. I wanted to be sure I was not running and had not been running my race in vain. Yet not even Titus, who was with me, was compelled to be circumcised, even though he was a Greek. This matter arose because some false believers had infiltrated our ranks to spy on the freedom we have in Christ Jesus and to make us slaves. We did not give in to them for a moment, so that the truth of the gospel might be preserved for you.

As for those who were held in high esteem – whatever they were makes no difference to me; God does not show favouritism – they added nothing to my message. On the contrary, they recognized that I had been entrusted with the task of preaching the gospel to the uncircumcised, just as Peter had been to the circumcised. For God, who was at work in Peter as an apostle to the circumcised, was also at work in me as an apostle to the Gentiles. James, Cephas and John, those esteemed as pillars, gave me and Barnabas the right hand of fellowship when they recognized the grace given to me. They agreed that we should go to the Gentiles, and they to the circumcised. All they asked was that we should continue to remember the poor, the very thing I had been eager to do all along.

When Cephas came to Antioch, I opposed him to his face, because he stood condemned. For before certain men came from James, he used to eat with the Gentiles. But when they arrived, he began to draw back and separate himself from the Gentiles because he was afraid of those who belonged to the circumcision group. The other Jews joined him in his hypocrisy, so that by their hypocrisy even Barnabas was led astray.

When I saw that they were not acting in line with the truth of the gospel, I said to Cephas in front of them all, "You are a Jew, yet you live like a Gentile and not like a Jew. How is it, then, that you force Gentiles to follow Jewish customs?

"We who are Jews by birth and not sinful Gentiles know that a person is not justified by the works of the law, but by faith in Jesus Christ. So we, too, have put our faith in Christ Jesus that we may be justified by faith in Christ and not by the works of the

> *law, because by the works of the law no one will be justified.*
>
> *"But if, in seeking to be justified in Christ, we Jews find ourselves also among the sinners, doesn't that mean that Christ promotes sin? Absolutely not! If I rebuild what I destroyed, then I really would be a lawbreaker.*
>
> *"For through the law I died to the law so that I might live for God. I have been crucified with Christ and I no longer live, but Christ lives in me. The life I now live in the body, I live by faith in the Son of God, who loved me and gave himself for me. I do not set aside the grace of God, for if righteousness could be gained through the law, Christ died for nothing!"*

> *But when the set time had fully come, God sent his Son, born of a woman, born under the law, to redeem those under the law, that we might receive adoption to sonship. Because you are his sons, God sent the Spirit of his Son into our hearts, the Spirit who calls out, "Abba, Father." So you are no longer a slave, but God's child; and since you are his child, God has made you also an heir.*

My childhood was brilliant. I had parents who loved God, and cared for me. Their passion was to invest their lives in their children for God's glory. I was taken to church at least twice every Sunday from nine months before my birth. Devout Christ-followers in that church prayed daily for my spiritual development.

Acceptance through performance

Growing up, I soon recognized that if I went to the services of this church, without complaining, my parents were very happy, and the church leaders very pleased. This wasn't difficult; I could count the ceiling tiles as well as the next child!

I was learning early that if I performed well, if I did what was expected of me, I would be accepted and appreciated. In my early teens, I had my first contact with Operation Mobilisation. Prayer meetings were a feature of the movement: long ones! It was immediately evident that, if I attended these prayer meetings, especially if I stayed to the end, that was credit in the bank. Giving out tracts to everyone you met was another area that was emphasised. So I went for it big time. On one bus that I caught regularly I gave everyone a tract. It was only later I realized that as it was the same bus each day, many of my fellow travellers were the same people, and must have quite a collection of tracts.

I learned that acceptance was based on performance. If I did everything I was expected to do, and if possible a little more, then rewards would follow. And we all live in a performance culture. What we do, what we achieve, is often the first thing we think of, to sum ourselves up. It is what our CVs are made up of, not just professionally, but even in our hobbies – Grade 8 guitar playing alongside running 10k or winning a debating competition. We live in a culture where performance and success are celebrated; positions, titles, and prosperity applauded.

Slave or child?

All of this can so easily trickle down to our relationship with God. "If I can do all those things which I believe God wants me to do, acceptance by Him will be guaranteed." You can imagine the result of this thinking for me: all the church services I could manage; the daily quiet time an absolute must; evangelism something I just had to do, and, and...

I had become an Evangelical slave. With my background, I knew my salvation was free, a gift of grace. But I struggled to live in grace. It was as though I felt I constantly had to perform to remain in God's good books. A slave has to do, to perform, to please his master. That was how I was living in my relationship with God. But I am a fallen human being. I never did what I felt to be necessary to my satisfaction, so there was no hope of my performance pleasing God. But it's a roundabout, and once you are on it, it's hard to jump off. As you keep trying harder, the roundabout speed increases, and so does the sense of failure and guilt.

Before their conversion, the Gentile believers in Galatia knew nothing of this roundabout. They had trusted Christ and found freedom in Him. But the leaders at the church in Jerusalem were not happy about their freedom.

Paul, who wrote this letter, knew all about this roundabout, and that remarkable statement "as for legalistic righteousness faultless" (Philippians 3:6) proves the point. But one wonderful day he had jumped off. He placed his faith in Christ who had perfectly fulfilled the Law on his behalf. Paul realized that Christ's sacrificial death had atoned before

God for his breaking of the Law. God's Spirit, now within him, gave him a desire to keep the Law. It no longer felt like a heavy weight, something he had to do. It was something he now wanted to do, in gratitude to the one who had done everything for him. The Holy Spirit within us moves us to follow God's decrees and to be careful to keep His laws (Ezekiel 36:27).

In Romans 8:2, Paul writes, "Through Christ Jesus the law of the Spirit of life set me free from the law of sin and death." That is what Paul had experienced and was so concerned for others to enjoy. Whereas previously life had been dominated by fear and legalism, now through the Holy Spirit, he knew there was "no condemnation" (verse 1) and absolute freedom.

You would imagine that anyone who came across Paul's message of freedom would be utterly delighted, and the more they had struggled to keep the Law, and the more important they had felt this to be, the more delightful this freedom would appear. But in fact, many were afraid of it. Surely Paul must be wrong? Surely God could not be sanctioning the abandonment of these rules and regulations for serving and approaching Him? They felt that Paul was doing away with the Law which had been from their earliest memory the basis of their lives. And they did not grasp just how powerful the crucifixion and resurrection had been, and what a change God had made in the way He wanted to be approached.

So the Jewish leaders head for Galatia to put things right. "We will stamp out this so-called freedom, and restore the trusted and tried, and very safe status quo."

The Galatians fell for it. Paul is astonished. "You foolish Galatians! Who has bewitched you?" (Galatians 3:1). J. B. Phillips paraphrases it as, "You dear idiots of Galatia." How difficult it is to continuously live in the experience of grace. There is a natural drift back to relying on ourselves, our efforts, and our performance. And there are plenty of people who will encourage us in that direction.

But what a choice they were making, to rely on their continuous work rather than on the finished work of Christ. It was to choose constant uncertainty and vulnerability. It was to go back under the daily weight of the Law, rather than enjoying the liberty of relationship with Christ. Foolishness indeed!

I have an almost desperate longing that Christians should appreciate all that they have in Christ. I love Paul's statement to the Colossians: "For in Christ all the fullness of the Deity lives in bodily form, and you have been given fullness in Christ" (Colossians 2:9–10). The Authorized Version finishes with the phrase, "and you are complete in him". All of God is in Christ and when Christ is in you, there is absolutely no need for anything additional. We have all that we need to thrive as Christians, to enjoy God and the life He has won for us through His Son.

But Paul immediately has to defend the statement he makes to the Colossians. "Therefore do not let anyone judge you by what you eat or drink, or with regard to a religious festival, a New Moon celebration or a Sabbath day" (Colossians 2:16). There were some people clearly snapping at the heels of the Colossian believers: "Do not handle! Do not taste! Do not touch!" (Colossians 2:21)

Paul knew all about such battles. He tells them in Galatians chapter two about his visit to Jerusalem when he took with him Barnabas and Titus. There would be no problem with Barnabas, a circumcised Jew, accompanying him, but what would they make of Titus, an uncircumcised Gentile? It does appear to have been a controversial visit. Some were intent on bringing Paul and his companions back into slavery (Galatians 2:4). There seems to have been a battle over Titus. Some wanted him circumcised. But Paul would not allow it. This was now a "gospel" issue for Paul. "We did not give in to them for a moment, so that the truth of the gospel might remain with you" (Galatians 2:5). When Titus left Jerusalem still uncircumcised, but now accepted as a brother in Christ, it was a great day for the gospel.

This was just one battle Paul had to fight to maintain Christian freedom. In the second half of chapter two, we move from Jerusalem to Antioch. The apostle Peter was there, and was having a good time of fellowship with Gentile believers in the city. He was treating them as equals, enjoying meals with them. Then some people came from Jerusalem. Peter's behaviour changes overnight. Now there is no eating with them. They are second-class citizens within the kingdom.

Paul is having none of it. This is such a serious issue, he opposes Peter to his face, publicly. "We may be Jews, but we have learned the hard way that a man is not justified by observing the law, but by faith in Jesus Christ. We have found freedom in Christ. Do you want to bring our Gentile brothers under the bondage we have been released from?" His knockout argument is in Galatians 2:21: "If righteousness could be gained through the law, Christ died for nothing."

It's that point which provokes the anger you see in Paul in Galatians 1. Paul is livid, and for good reason. This adding to the simplicity of the gospel actually destroys the gospel, and the end result of it is the conclusion that "Christ died for nothing." A message which adds works to grace is "really no gospel at all" (Galatians 1:7). You can see the message from the Jerusalem visitors in Acts 15:1: "Some men came down from Judea to Antioch and were teaching the brothers: 'Unless you are circumcised, according to the custom taught by Moses, you cannot be saved.'" So they were not decrying faith in Christ, they were adding to it. Theirs was a "Jesus plus" message. It's anathema to Paul, and anyone who preaches it should be eternally condemned.

Why is he so strong? Remember what he wrote to the Colossians: "You are complete in him" (Colossians 2:10, AV). This detracts from Christ's glory, as well as calling into question the sufficiency of His work at the cross.

The truth of the matter is: "When the time arrived that was set by God the Father, God sent his Son, born among us of a woman, born under the conditions of the law so that he might redeem those of us who have been kidnapped by the law. Thus we have been set free to experience our rightful heritage. You can tell for sure that you are now fully adopted as his own children because God sent the Spirit of his Son into our lives crying out, 'Papa! Father!' Doesn't that privilege of intimate conversation with God make it plain that you are not a slave, but a child? And if you are a child, you're also an heir, with complete access to the inheritance." (Galatians 4:4–7, *The Message*).

It was the seventh verse of Galatians 4 that set me free from my Evangelical slavery. In my late teens I realized that I had been "doing" to please God. This verse showed me that God couldn't be more pleased with me, because I was His child. After this utterly transforming revelation I found that I still did most of the things I had been previously doing, but it was all so different. No longer was I doing these things to please. That is the difference between a slave and a son or daughter. A slave works to please the master. If the master isn't pleased, the consequences may be grave. It is a life of uncertainty, vulnerability, and fear. But the child in a loving home knows their identity as a child is sufficient. He or she is not working to please; acceptance because of relationship is guaranteed and complete. The motive for service is now gratitude for all that God had done for me in Christ.

So it is vital that we stand tall on this rock of our complete acceptance as children in a family where the Father is perfect in His love for His children. "It is for freedom that Christ has set us free. Stand firm, then, and do not let yourselves be burdened again by a yoke of slavery" (Galatians 5:1).

Everything gone but the rock is solid

Read Job 1 – 2:10 and 42:1–6.

If ever a man lost all the identity definers we normally rely on, it was Job. He had everything. He had his integrity. "This man was blameless and upright; he feared God and shunned evil" (Job 1:1). He had family: seven sons and three daughters (verse 2). He had known success and had wealth. "He owned seven thousand sheep, three thousand camels, five hundred yoke of oxen and five hundred donkeys, and had a large number of servants" (verse 3).

He lost everything and it seems it was almost overnight. First he lost his servants, then his wealth, then his family (Job 1:13–20). In the chapters that follow, his so-called friends constantly attack his integrity; Job would have benefitted far more from their silence than their attempts at counselling! He was "the greatest man among all the people of the East" (Job 1:3) and became "a man in whose face people spit" (Job 17:6).

However do you survive such disasters? Certainly not without a monumental struggle. Job got so low he wished he had never been born (Job 10:18–19). But somehow he held on. God calls Job His servant. This is a term which implies a very special relationship. It is, for example, how God refers to Moses. Job's friends seem determined to destroy this special relationship. At times as you read the book you feel there is no hope of its survival. But every now and then there are glimpses of the trust in that special relationship enduring. "Though he slay me, yet will I hope in him" (Job 13:15). "I know that my Redeemer lives, and that in the end he will stand upon the earth. And after my skin has been destroyed, yet in my flesh I will see God; I myself will see him with my own eyes – I, and not another. How my heart yearns within me!" (Job 19:25–27). In his darkness, Job has a glimpse of something or someone who one day will put everything right. In the uncertainty, there remain some things of which he can say, "I know." And there is another vital thing he knows: "But he knows the way that I take; when he has tested me, I shall come forth as gold" (Job 23:10).

This is the thrilling faith in adversity of Job, God's servant. It is also the contention of this book that, if you are firm and sure of your identity in Christ, the most violent storms of life are navigable.

As I write, my mind goes to a person who struggles to even attend a church communion service, because of a constant energy-sapping feeling of unworthiness. The memory of a particular sin committed prior to conversion is a constant torment. He understands the theology. He has repented of this sin, probably many times! He knows that the finished work of Christ atones for that particular sin, along with all his other sins. But emotionally he cannot embrace the truth that he is intellectually convinced of. Satan is a freedom robber, and shame is one of his most potent weapons.

Many years ago I was in Rio de Janeiro. I got up on a Sunday morning to go for an early jog. As I left my host's home, there were a number of roads I could have followed. One led up a hill and, in the distance, I could see a number of small lights burning. I decided to go and investigate. When I came close to the lights, I saw they were candles placed on tablecloths on the roadside. On the tablecloths there was quality food spread, and the dogs of Rio were having a party! When I got back to the house, I asked my host what it was all about. He explained that this was an offering made mostly by the poor, who could least afford it, to give away their food to the spirits. Would their offering appease the anger of the spirits?

God is rightly angry with us about our sins. But *all* of that anger has been poured out on His holy Son. The cup of His wrath has been poured out completely. He is no longer angry with me, however angry I may become with myself for my many failures and sins.

CHAPTER FIVE

Ball and Chain

Read Romans 8:31–39:

> *What, then, shall we say in response to these things? If God is for us, who can be against us? He who did not spare his own Son, but gave him up for us all – how will he not also, along with him, graciously give us all things? Who will bring any charge against those whom God has chosen? It is God who justifies. Who then is the one who condemns? No one. Christ Jesus who died – more than that, who was raised to life – is at the right hand of God and is also interceding for us. Who shall separate us from the love of Christ? Shall trouble or hardship or persecution or famine or nakedness or danger or sword? As it is written:*
>
> *"For your sake we face death all day long;*
> *we are considered as sheep to be slaughtered."*
>
> *No, in all these things we are more than conquerors through him who loved us. For I am convinced that*

> *neither death nor life, neither angels nor demons, neither the present nor the future, nor any powers, neither height nor depth, nor anything else in all creation, will be able to separate us from the love of God that is in Christ Jesus our Lord.*

In the brilliant story of *The Lion King*, we meet the young lion cub, Simba, the son of the powerful king of the Pride Lands. As the king's son he has status and security. But it is not long before he is racked with guilt. Simba believes his father is killed because of him, as he attempts to save Simba from a stampede of wildebeest.

Overwhelmed by grief through the death of his father, he is confronted by his uncle, Scar, a dark satanic figure who accuses Simba of being responsible for his father's death. In desperate grief and shame, Simba cries out in confusion, unsure what he should do. Scar advises he run away and never come back. It is a temptation that so many struggling with guilt grapple with. "Don't face it. Push it under the carpet, and the feelings of guilt and shame will pass. Just give it time."

The young lion born to be king is driven by guilt into loneliness. It appears his rightful inheritance is lost forever. But it's a story with a happy ending! A childhood friend meets him years later and persuades him to return to the Pride Lands and rescue them from the dreadful consequences of Scar's rule. It's not easy to persuade Simba. The years have passed, but the guilt hasn't. He is still blaming himself for his dad's death. The constant battle with guilt has destroyed any sense of worth. Even though he is now a full-grown lion, Simba feels wholly inadequate and thoroughly scared at the prospect of returning. He meets a wise baboon who knew his father. Simba thinks the baboon is crazy and asks who he is. But the baboon turns this question around and asks Simba to consider his own identity.

The baboon advises Simba that if he looks closely he will see his father living in him. He takes Simba to a pool and shows him his reflection. As Simba looks in, he sees the likeness of his father staring back at him. Then he hears his father's voice reassurung him that his identity as the king's son still outweighs Simba's actions or experiences.

It's what he needs to know. It is sufficient to send him back to the Pride Lands to claim his rightful inheritance.

The brother I referred to at the close of the last chapter feels he lives life with a ball and chain around his leg. The memory of this past sin constantly drags him down. In his happiest moments Satan brings this memory to his mind. In his most successful moments "the big failure" steals his joy. In those moments when he is unhappy, Satan again brings this memory to him, truly kicking him when he is already down. Shame is a devastating, spiritually debilitating, truly devilish thing. Tragically it is also a common thing. Charles Swindoll writes, "Most folk it seems are better acquainted with their guilt and shame than with their God." What a victory for the evil one.

Running restrictions

Living with shame is like running the race of life constantly looking over your shoulder. That is a bumpy, painful, and slow way to run. The writer of the epistle to the Hebrews is very clear where our eyes should be fixed as we run this race – our eyes should be fixed on Jesus (Hebrews 12:2). It is interesting that the writer continues, "Jesus… who for the joy set before him endured the cross, scorning its shame, and sat down at the right hand of the throne of God." Jesus dealt with our shame at the cross. Then He sat down – work done, shame forever dealt with.

But sadly many, though they agree with that truth intellectually, cannot rest emotionally. The torment of the memory of past sin grinds on. It is as if someone has a finger on the rewind button of their lives. But the tape is mangled and the only bits it replays are those moments of sin and failure. And every so often, it sticks and one particular sin is replayed, over and over again. The finger on the rewind button is not the finger of God!

This strategy of shame is not a new thing. It is as old as humanity. "Then the man and his wife heard the sound of the Lord God as he was walking in the garden in the cool of the day, and they hid from the Lord God among the trees of the garden. But the Lord God called to the man, 'Where are you?' He answered, 'I heard you in the garden, and I was afraid because I was naked; so I hid'" (Genesis 3:8–10).

What a total and dreadful transformation. Eden had been a shame-free place. "The man and his wife were both naked, and they felt no shame" (Genesis 2:25). But the moment they sinned, "the eyes of both of them were opened, and they realized they were naked; so they sewed fig leaves together and made coverings for themselves" (Genesis 3:7). Next minute they are hiding from God (Genesis 3:8). Shame had become a reality which we have wrestled with ever since, and it has become a favourite weapon in our enemy's toolkit.

Remarkably, Satan has been so successful that, today, feelings of guilt and shame are often associated with religion. But again, this is nothing new. Jesus said of the Pharisees, "Woe to you [or shame on you], because you load people down with burdens they can hardly carry, and you yourselves will not lift one finger to help them" (Luke 11:46). Whenever religion becomes works-based, it inevitably leads to a sense of failure, guilt, and shame. Preachers present the Sermon on the Mount as the standard we must live by if we are to please God. It is not long before we are feeling utter failures. Guilt and shame sweep in.

But the people who say they have embraced the message of grace can still leave many believers feeling they just don't make the grade. We have ways of making people feel that the way *we* worship, the way *we* pray, the way *we* preach – these are the only true ways. And if those ways just do not do it for others, then those others must be, in some way, deeply spiritually deficient.

It's time to rest!

The invitation of Jesus was not to keep a long list of "Do's" and "Don'ts". His invitation was, "Come to me, all you who are weary and burdened, and I will give you *rest*. Take my yoke upon you and learn from me, for I am gentle and humble in heart, and you will find *rest* for your souls. For my yoke is easy and my burden is light" (Matthew 11:28–30). William Hendriksen writes, "In Jewish literature a 'yoke' represented the sum total of obligations which according to the teaching of the rabbis a person must take upon himself."[5]

As we know, by misinterpreting and adding to the Law, Israel's teachers had placed an unbearably impossible burden on the people (Acts 15:10). Now Jesus says, "Take my yoke." He is saying, "Take the sum total of the obligations I place upon you. What are those obligations? Just one. Trust only and completely in me for your salvation. I have fulfilled all the obligations entirely to my Father's satisfaction. All that remains for you is total trust in me and in what I have done on your behalf. So 'come to me,' don't go to anyone or anything else. Don't try and do anything else." No wonder Jesus adds, "My yoke is easy and my burden is light" (Matthew 11:30).

Shame is the very opposite of this lightness and restfulness. Lewes Smedes writes, "Shame is a very heavy feeling. It's a feeling that we do not measure up and maybe never will measure up to the sorts of people we are meant to be. The feeling, when we are conscious of it, gives us a vague

---

5 William Hendriksen, *New Testament Commentary: Matthew*, Edinburgh: Banner of Truth, 1974, page 504.

disgust with ourselves which in turn feels like a hunk of lead in our hearts. Unhealthy shame spills over everything we are it flops, sloshes and smears our whole being."[6]

It is so true that shame can smear our whole being. We can never get away from its hold over us. Soon we begin to build our identity around it. Yes, we sinned and that sin was wrong. Satan then suggests that not just the sin is wrong, but we must be all wrong. We must be useless and worthless individuals.

Read 1 Samuel chapter 12.

Samuel is growing old and he appoints his sons to be his successors, serving as judges for Israel. But they are nothing like Samuel. They don't "walk in his ways" (1 Samuel 8:3). The elders of Israel call a meeting and the result of the meeting is a request to Samuel: "Appoint a king to lead us" (verse 4). There was nothing wrong with that in principle, as long as they kept to the clear guidelines God gave them at the time (Deuteronomy 17:14–21). There was however no turning to God to ask Him for a solution to this problem. They immediately turned to a structural solution, and they clearly had it in mind to be like all the nations around them, who had their own kings. The leaders realize their failure when God sends thunder and rain on the land at the time you would least expect it, wheat harvest time (1 Samuel 12:17). This really gets the attention of the people. "So all the people stood in awe of the Lord and of Samuel" (verse 18).

---

6 Lewis Smedes, *Shame and Grace: Healing the Shame We Don't Deserve*, San Francisco: Harper San Francisco, 1993, page 5.

They appeal to Samuel to pray for them "that we will not die" (verse 19). God's word through Samuel reveals His amazing mercy: "'Do not be afraid,' Samuel replied. 'You have done all this evil; yet do not turn away from the Lord, but serve the Lord with all your heart'" (verse 20).

> Dale Ralph Davis comments, "Do you see it? You don't go back and wallow in your guilt, relive the tragic mistake, the 'big one' that has soured your life. You don't make yourself miserable by bathing your mind in the memory of your rebellion, punching the replay button and going over the whole messy episode in lurid and precise detail as though such misery makes atonement. No, you go forward in basic, simple fidelity to Yahweh from that point on."[7]

The covenant is not broken. The relationship with God holds firm, though clouded by rebellion and needing to be attended to through confession and repentance. The rock remains. It is interesting that the Children of Israel appeal to Samuel to pray for them so that they will not die. What a picture of the risen Lord Jesus who "speaks to the Father in our defence" (1 John 2:1) and "always lives to intercede for" us (Hebrews 7:25).

Whom will you believe?

We have some decisions to make. Are we going to believe the lies that our enemy speaks over us, or the truth that our Father

7 Dale Ralph Davis, *1 Samuel: Looking on the Heart*, Fearn: Christian Focus, 2008, page 102.

seeks to impress upon us by His Holy Spirit? The only way to deal with the constant undermining of shame is to choose every day, and probably many times every day, to believe the truth of what God our Father says about us. We must learn to talk to ourselves. You may have been told it's the first sign of madness, but in the battle, it is an essential weapon. We must constantly remind ourselves of it. Personally, sometimes I have to voice it out loud: "Satan, you are a liar. God's verdict on me is the very opposite of your accusations." If we don't learn to agree with God, we will find ourselves running the race of life constantly looking back over our shoulders, and with lead weights around our ankles.

CHAPTER SIX

Snow White

Read Psalm 51:

Have mercy on me, O God,
according to your unfailing love;
according to your great compassion
blot out my transgressions.
Wash away all my iniquity
and cleanse me from my sin.

For I know my transgressions,
and my sin is always before me.
Against you, you only, have I sinned
and done what is evil in your sight;
so you are right in your verdict
and justified when you judge.
Surely I was sinful at birth,
sinful from the time my mother conceived me.
Yet you desired faithfulness even in the womb;
you taught me wisdom in that secret place.

Cleanse me with hyssop, and I shall be clean;
wash me, and I shall be whiter than snow.
Let me hear joy and gladness;
let the bones you have crushed rejoice.
Hide your face from my sins
and blot out all my iniquity.

Create in me a pure heart, O God,
and renew a steadfast spirit within me.
Do not cast me from your presence
or take your Holy Spirit from me.
Restore to me the joy of your salvation
and grant me a willing spirit, to sustain me.

Then I will teach transgressors your ways,
so that sinners will turn back to you.
Deliver me from the guilt of bloodshed, O God,
you who are God my Saviour,
and my tongue will sing of your righteousness.
Open my lips, Lord,
and my mouth will declare your praise.
You do not delight in sacrifice, or I would bring it;
you do not take pleasure in burnt offerings.
My sacrifice, O God, is a broken spirit;
a broken and contrite heart
you, God, will not despise.

May it please you to prosper Zion,
to build up the walls of Jerusalem.

Then you will delight in the sacrifices of the righteous,
in burnt offerings offered whole;
then bulls will be offered on your altar.

Winston Churchill said of Clement Atlee: "He is a very humble man, with a great deal to be humble about." You might be thinking; "My shame is real and I have a great deal to be shameful about." I can understand that feeling. We hear a lot today about guilt feelings, and how unhealthy they can be, but we know we have a great deal of real guilt, not just guilt feelings.

Releasing the ball and chain

Let's watch a man dealing with very real guilt, and getting to the place of freedom and joy after grievous sin. David had enjoyed seventeen years of unqualified success on the battlefield as king of Israel. He was known as a man who "enquired of the Lord" before he took any action. Some believe it was a moment of overconfidence when he sent out his troops under Joab's command and remained at home resting. Others think that, after seventeen years of battle, he thoroughly deserved a rest. Whatever the reason for the decision, it proved to be tragic. Resting at home, he observes beautiful Bathsheba bathing. His lust is ignited through the indiscipline of his eyes, and in no time adultery with Bathsheba is followed by planning her husband's murder.

Nine months pass, and the baby conceived through this adulterous relationship is born. David has been living with specific unconfessed sin, and it has taken its toll. Many people think his words recorded in Psalm 32 were written during this nine-month period: "When I kept silent, my bones wasted away through my groaning all day long. For day and night your hand was heavy upon me; my strength was sapped as in the heat of summer." In his great psalm of repentance, he writes about his bones being crushed (Psalm 51:8).

If there is anyone reading this who knows that bone-crushing, strength-sapping feeling of living with unconfessed sin, let's deal with it now. David deals with it through the intervention of a friend. Nathan is used by God to help David see the unconfessed sin in his life, and the kind of man he has become through that unconfessed sin. Nathan raises the issue of David's sin through a story. There is a rich man and a poor man in the story. The rich man has a large flock of sheep and many cattle. The poor man has nothing apart from one ewe lamb. This lamb meant everything to him. In fact it is described as being "like a daughter to him" (2 Samuel 12:3). A traveller arrives at the rich man's home. Instead of taking one of the many sheep from his own flock to prepare him a meal, he steals the poor man's one ewe lamb.

When David hears this story, we are told he "burned with anger" (2 Samuel 12:5). He probably thinks Nathan is relating a real incident, and one of his subjects is coming to him looking for justice. It was a mean and horrible thing for this rich man to do. However, David's reaction seems over the top. "As surely as the Lord lives, the man who did this must die!" (2 Samuel 12:5). When we live with unconfessed sin we can become very hard and very unforgiving of the sins of others. The law covered this sort of incident, as David goes on to point out. The thief should have paid for the lamb four times over (Exodus 22:1). David's call for the death penalty shows that something was dying within David, as he lived with this sin unconfessed.

The wonderful thing about David is that when Nathan shows him that *he* is the rich man who had many wives and concubines, and yet stole Bathsheba from someone much poorer than him, his repentance is immediate and total. He does not minimize his sin in any way. Look at the words he uses in Psalm 51: "my transgressions" (verse 1); "my iniquity" and "my sin" (verse 2); "evil" (verse 4). His language in verse 7 shows that this sin has made him feel dirty and unclean. It has replaced his joy with sadness (verse 8). His normally steadfast spirit has been weakened (verse 10). Crucially he appreciates that he has sinned against God (verse 4). He has sinned grievously against Bathsheba and Uriah, but supremely his sin, as with all sin, is against God whose commandments he has broken, and in whose image Bathsheba and Uriah were made.

I remember a young man who came to see me, whose sin had become public knowledge. He was broken. He explained how he had shamed his family, ruined his career prospects, and let himself and so many others down. But I had to point out to him that in the list there was no mention either of the victim of the crime he had committed, or of God, whose name he had dishonoured. David makes no excuses; indeed, he justifies God: "You are right in your verdict and justified when you judge" (verse 4).

The seventh verse of this psalm is remarkable and terrific in the light of all this: "Cleanse me with hyssop, and I shall be clean; wash me, and I shall be whiter than snow." David has committed adultery and planned murder, and as we have seen he fully understands the seriousness of his sin, yet he believes he can be washed clean. He can have a cleanliness that is whiter than virgin snow.

God, through the prophet Isaiah, says to His rebellious people, "'Come now, let us reason together,' says the Lord. 'Though your sins are like scarlet, they shall be as white as snow; though they are red as crimson, they shall be like wool'" (Isaiah 1:18). With a Father like that encouraging us to return to Him, how can we go on living another moment with unconfessed sin? However frequent our sin may have been, however serious we may consider it to be, there is complete cleansing available. Redemption is available to all repentant sinners through a slain lamb "without blemish or defect" (1 Peter 1:19).

Character

How could David be so confident of this? How can you and I be equally confident? As you look at this psalm, it's clear that David's confidence was based on a number of convictions. He had a deep conviction about the character of God. He knows as he repents he is coming before a God of unfailing love and great compassion (Psalm 51:1). As we have seen, he has already acknowledged the justice of God in verse 4. This perfect balance in the character of God was clearly a great comfort to David. I am afraid when my children were growing up that the response when they came to me over an issue might be highly variable. It would have depended to some degree on how I was feeling on the day that they came. There is no such uncertainty or need for any sense of vulnerability when we come before God. However we come, rejoicing in success, or broken in repentance, whenever we come, day or night, Sunday morning or Monday morning, the response will always be consistent with His perfect character. He "does not change like shifting shadows" (James 1:17).

If you have decided as you are reading this book that you are going to deal with unconfessed sin, I want you to be absolutely sure of the God you are approaching. He will deal justly with you, never minimizing your sin, and yet He will treat you with unfailing love. Many have a totally false view of God. Charles Swindoll writes, "Many Christians live their lives as though they expect to be examined by God once a year. God stands there frowning with his hand stuck in the pockets of his robe." He adds, "It's interesting how most people think of God in a robe."

If anyone should know what God is like, it is surely His eternal Son. Possibly the most famous story Jesus told was to help us understand the heart of His father. The prodigal son had blown his father's hard-earned inheritance. Demanding his part of the inheritance while his father was still alive was tantamount to wishing his dad dead before his time. Now the

Prodigal's on the way home, struggling with his identity on the journey, unsure of the welcome he will receive. "I am a son, but surely after what I have done, the best I can hope for is to be a servant in the house."

But the father he meets is a waiting father. It seems he has been waiting, longing for his son's return, since the day he left. He is also a running father, running to meet his son the moment he recognizes him. He is a forgiving, accepting, restoring father. The welcome is emotional and total. There is never a question about the Prodigal being anything other than a forgiven son, as he acknowledges his sin to his father. That is the picture the Lord Jesus gives us of His father. It was this understanding of God which gave David the confidence to approach Him in repentance after his awful failures. The word translated as "compassion" in verse 1 is an emotional term speaking of the tender warmth of God.

Covenant

David had a second conviction which gave him confidence at this time. The words "unfailing love" in verse 1 are covenant words. Even after these sins, David is convinced that he still belongs. The covenant is not broken by his failures. The prodigal son felt unworthy any longer to be called a son, but a son he remained. The covenants of God are as unshakeable as the character of God. His covenant promises are not in any way based on my performance, but entirely on His commitment to me. Horatius Bonar captured this beautifully with his words:

The clouds may go and come.
The storms may sweep my sky.
This blood-sealed friendship changes not.
The cross is ever nigh.

My wife, Win, and I are committed to one another for the rest of our lives by a covenant made in the sight of God and in the hearing of many witnesses. Words we used as we made that covenant express the fact that this commitment is to hold, even if circumstances may radically change. Words such as "in sickness or in health". I will let you into a secret. Win and I have had the occasional "spat" in over forty years of marriage. If we are foolish enough not to immediately deal with the spat it can cloud our relationship. Talking to one another for example can be more difficult for a time; even being in each other's company can become uncomfortable. But ending the relationship never crosses our minds. We are committed by unbreakable covenant. Our covenant is a very poor example compared with God's covenant with us. Sin can cloud our relationship with God, until it's dealt with. I don't think David wrote any worship psalms during the period he lived with unconfessed sin. Sin can make us feel uncomfortable in God's presence until we deal with it. But there is absolutely no way that sin will ever break the covenant. That is why David could return to God with such confidence. He knew the character of God, and the covenant of God.

> "But what happens if and when I sin?" you may ask. "Do I then forfeit my sonship and cease to be God's

> child?" No. Think of... a human family. Imagine a boy being offensively rude to his parents... Father and son are not on speaking terms... Has the boy ceased to be a son? No. Their relationship is just the same; it is their fellowship that has been broken. Relationship depends on birth; fellowship depends on behaviour. As soon as the boy apologizes, he is forgiven. And forgiveness restores fellowship. Meanwhile, his relationship has remained the same...
>
> And this applies also to us.[8]

Cross

Thirdly, David was convinced that God had provided the means by which he could enjoy cleansing. "Cleanse me with hyssop" (Psalm 51:7). When the Children of Israel had to apply the blood of the Passover lamb to their lintels and doorposts, if they were to escape death as God's judgment fell on Egypt, they did so with a bunch of hyssop (Exodus 12:22). The Mosaic Law provided no forgiveness for adultery or deliberate murder. The death penalty was inevitable. There was only one hope, the blood of sacrifice.

And so it is with us:

My hope is built on nothing less than Jesus'
blood and righteousness.
I dare not trust the sweetest frame, but wholly
lean on Jesus' name.

8 John Stott, *Basic Christianity* (rev. ed.), London: Inter-Varsity Press, 1971, page 135.

His oath, his covenant, his blood support me in the whelming flood.
When all around my soul gives way, He then is all my hope and stay.

The apostle Peter, referring to Jesus, writes, "he himself bore our sins in his body on the cross, so that we might die to sins and live for righteousness; by his wounds you have been healed" (1 Peter 2:24). Jesus is the means God has provided so that we can know cleansing today; complete cleansing from all our sin and shame. And it is at the cross where we find our true identity, our absolute security, and our true worth. Here we discover our new identity and the value that God places upon us. No longer do we need to go looking inside ourselves for self-esteem. The value that God places upon us is the life of His only Son.

Complete

But it was not just cleansing that David experienced. He looked to God for complete restoration, restoration of his previously steadfast spirit (Psalm 51:10), of his joy (verse 12), and to effective ministry (verse 13). Satan suggests after sinful failure there is no possibility of forgiveness: "You have gone too far this time. That is one failure too many." If he fails to win that battle, his next attempt is to suggest, "There can be no way back. You will never be the same again, never have that same spirit, that same desire to live for God's pleasure. You will never have that same joy, and that is certainly the end of your ministry." But there is absolutely no need for that to be the case. Reject the enemy's lies. The means for your forgiveness and restoration is more than adequate. It is perfect, and complete: it is none other than Jesus.

As I write these paragraphs, news reaches me of another pastor of a megachurch who has resigned following moral failure. This is tragic, potentially hugely kingdom-damaging, and, I am sure you agree, far too common. However, the report had some element of hope. It seems he resigned immediately after he fell, with no excuses and total repentance. The church leaders reported, "He will be focussing his full attention on his personal relationship with God and with his family. The governing body of the church is providing counsellors and ministers who will help guide him through the process of full repentance, cleansing and restoration." It's a tragedy, but that is at least a great start in dealing with it.

David is a brilliant example of how sin and shame, even the sin and shame of adultery and murder, can be cleansed, and healed. "By his wounds we are healed" (Isaiah 53:5).

Standing right alongside David is another servant of God who hit failure, but what a different story that is. Saul had a privileged start to life. His father Kish was "a man of standing". He probably had wealth and influence. Saul himself had impressive physical attributes. He was "a head taller than any of the others". In fact he was "without equal among the Israelites" (1 Samuel 9:2). Beyond all this, however, God had chosen and anointed him to be ruler of Israel (1 Samuel 9:17; 10:1). Early in Saul's career, there were signs of decisive and compassionate leadership (1 Samuel 11:4–8, 12–13).

It all started so well. But let's do what you are not supposed to do. Let's go to the last page of the book of Saul's life and see where it all ends up. He is killed on the battlefield, his body is fastened to the wall of Beth Shan, and his armour placed in the temple of the Ashtoreths (1 Samuel 31:10). So he ends up being a symbol of victory, not for God, but for God's enemies, who could crow over the fallen Saul – and the God he had claimed to serve. How are the mighty fallen, and fallen so far? If you study his life you will see a number of reasons for this disastrous end, and one you will surely not miss is his seemingly total inability to repent. Saul just couldn't voice the words, "I was wrong."

When Saul moves against the Amalekites, God's instructions could not have been clearer. "Now go, attack the Amalekites and totally destroy everything that belongs to them" (1 Samuel 15:3). Saul spares "the best of the sheep and cattle, the fat calves and lambs – everything that was good" (verse 9). When Samuel comes to Saul, Saul has the temerity to say, "I have carried out the Lord's instructions." Samuel's response says it all. "What then is this bleating of sheep in my ears?" (verse 14). Saul's immediate response to Samuel's challenge is to blame his soldiers, and to seek to spiritualize his failure (verse 15). Two men are both succeeding in their calling. Both hit dreadful failure. One – David – seeks the cleansing and renewal of the Lord in repentance. The other – Saul – just can't bring himself to do so.

The message of the New Testament is just as clear. I

love the way the good shepherd goes about the restoring of Peter. His denial of Jesus could hardly have been more definite. Look at Peter's denial of Jesus. "'You aren't one of his disciples too, are you?' she asked Peter. He replied, 'I am not'" (John 18:17). "So they asked him, 'You aren't one of his disciples too, are you?' He denied it, saying, 'I am not'" (verse 25). "'Didn't I see you with him in the garden?' Again Peter denied it, and at that moment a cock began to crow" (verse 26–27). After such a forceful declaration of devotion (Matthew 26:33–35), is there any way back from such blatant denial, uttered at the moment of our Lord's greatest need?

The particular concern for Peter after Jesus' resurrection is seen in those two great words, "and Peter", in Mark 16:7. The women who were the first witnesses of His resurrection were instructed, "But go, tell his disciples and Peter." It is surely interesting that only Mark records these words. It is widely believed that Peter's memories were the source of Mark's writings.

Jesus is perfectly prepared for Peter to feel the pain of his denials in order to get him back to where He wants him to be. He doesn't just gloss over them. Peter must face what he has done. As the cock crowed, Luke records, "The Lord turned and looked straight at Peter" (Luke 22:61). That look must have gone right to Peter's heart. It is hard to imagine the emotions it must have generated in him. But there was grace in the look, and grace in the fact that Jesus only *looked*. He did not *speak*. One word of recognition from Jesus to Peter at that moment, and it would have been clear to everyone that Peter's denials were blatant lies.

Peter's denials took place around a charcoal fire. Jesus chooses another charcoal fire to restore and recommission Peter (John 21:9). Three times Peter had specifically denied his discipleship. Three times Jesus asks, "Do you love me?" The first time He asks the question, He adds, "more than these". He is almost certainly referring to the other disciples. Peter must face the claim he had made that he was different. He had boldly stated, "Even if all fall away, I will not" (Mark 14:29). From here on, through the honest, sensitive pastoral care of the good shepherd, Peter's love and commitment will be without reserve, and his ministry truly crucial to the founding of the church. Although he later disagrees with Paul, of course, and is publicly rebuked by him. But Peter is happy for his failures to go on record – it is believed he was the source of much of Mark's Gospel. So presumably he wanted the "warts and all" picture to be in there. The result, for us, is that Peter is probably the most human of all the apostles, the one we would recognize if we met him, the one we can identify with most closely.

John 21 is interesting. It certainly reads like an appendix to the Gospel. The final two verses of the previous chapter appear to bring the Gospel to a close. Some believe that this chapter was added later, either by John or by one of his close colleagues. But if it is original, why did John include it? Was one reason just to show to us how concerned Jesus is to see those who fail restored and recommissioned? It is wonderful that Peter wasn't just forgiven and then side-lined. He could forever after have been seen as damaged goods, never to be really trusted again. But instead he was forgiven, restored, recommissioned and took his vital place as one of the most significant leaders in the early days of the church.

CHAPTER SEVEN

God's Masterpiece

Read Psalm 139:

You have searched me, Lord,
and you know me.
You know when I sit and when I rise;
you perceive my thoughts from afar.
You discern my going out and my lying down;
you are familiar with all my ways.
Before a word is on my tongue
you, Lord, know it completely.
You hem me in behind and before,
and you lay your hand upon me.
Such knowledge is too wonderful for me,
too lofty for me to attain.

Where can I go from your Spirit?
Where can I flee from your presence?
If I go up to the heavens, you are there;
if I make my bed in the depths, you are there.

If I rise on the wings of the dawn,
if I settle on the far side of the sea,
even there your hand will guide me,
your right hand will hold me fast.
If I say, "Surely the darkness will hide me
and the light become night around me,"
even the darkness will not be dark to you;
the night will shine like the day,
for darkness is as light to you.

For you created my inmost being;
you knit me together in my mother's womb.
I praise you because I am fearfully and
wonderfully made;
your works are wonderful,
I know that full well.
My frame was not hidden from you
when I was made in the secret place,
when I was woven together in the depths of
the earth.
Your eyes saw my unformed body;
all the days ordained for me were written
in your book
before one of them came to be.
How precious to me are your thoughts, God!
How vast is the sum of them!
Were I to count them,
they would outnumber the grains of sand –
when I awake, I am still with you.

If only you, God, would slay the wicked!
Away from me, you who are bloodthirsty!
They speak of you with evil intent;
your adversaries misuse your name.
Do I not hate those who hate you, Lord,
and abhor those who are in rebellion against you?
I have nothing but hatred for them;
I count them my enemies.
Search me, God, and know my heart;
test me and know my anxious thoughts.
See if there is any offensive way in me,
and lead me in the way everlasting.

Many people in this country and others are fascinated by personality quizzes, or the longer, more scientifically based Myers–Briggs personality analysis. We want to know if we are introverts, extroverts, or whatever the study promises to tell us. We are often fascinated by knowing and understanding ourselves – and when we meet new friends, or fall in love, we often want to know these new people as well and as deeply as we possibly can. But our knowledge will never be more than patchy, when compared to what God knows about us.

God knows

God knows us inside out. David reflects on this in his much-loved Psalm 139. What was true of David is true of me. "O Lord, you have searched me and you know me" (verse 1).

The idea in the word translated as "searched" is taking a spade and digging deep. The Lord has dug down deep into my life, turned it all over, and examined it. He knows when I sit and when I rise; even my innermost thoughts which I can hide from everyone else are an open book to Him (verse 2). I have a problem. Sometimes my mouth moves faster than my brain! I find I have started a sentence but I have no idea where it's going, or how I am going to bring it in to land: "Before a word is on my tongue you know it completely, O Lord" (verse 4). However, this can be understood in a second way: "When there is no word on my tongue, you know it completely, O Lord." Some wear their emotions on their sleeve. You know exactly what they are thinking and feeling at any given time. Others would make far better poker players. You never quite know what they are thinking or feeling, and they reveal little or nothing. Sometimes the reserve and apparent calm appear so "spiritual". When there is no word on my tongue, but I am ranting and raging inside, "You, Lord, know it completely."

And He has known us from the very beginning; not just known us, but actually formed us. He made us, He wove us together. You are created by God. You are His handiwork (Ephesians 2:10). You are one of God's masterpieces, one of His works of art, and His signature is on every picture. You are made in His image and likeness. This is true of our creation, and our re-creation or salvation.

God delights

God delights in and likes to display His masterpieces. Listen to His delight in His faithful servant Job. He says to Satan, "Have you considered my servant Job? There is no one on earth like him; he is blameless and upright, a man who fears God and shuns evil" (Job 1:8). At the beginning of chapter two, I wrote that when we are thinking about life, its purpose and meaning, we must start at the right place. We must ask the question, "Why did God create us?" The masterpiece displays the artist's skill. We were made to display God's glory. Surely the authors of the Westminster Catechism got it right when they wrote, "Man's chief end is to glorify God and enjoy him forever." A masterpiece today may have many copies, but you are the original, "one of a kind" masterpiece. He knit you together in your mother's womb. You are "fearfully and wonderfully made" by Him (Psalm 139:14). Every aspect of your body and your personality is His design.

But, you may say, my body has been affected by genetic inheritance, and as the years pass, it's being affected ever more rapidly by ageing. The wear and tear is obvious for all to see. Yet God knew all about those effects when He created you. He took it all into account. He made you in such a way that you would make a unique contribution to the promotion of His glory, and He makes no mistakes. "God saw all that he had made, and it was very good" (Genesis 1:31). God's creation, including you and me, was and is exactly as He wanted it to be. You can relax and be yourself; you don't need to be constantly striving to be like someone else. Someone once said, "If you spend all your life trying to be someone else, who is going to be you?"

> "Be yourself; everyone else is already taken." – *Oscar Wilde*
>
> "Be yourself – not your idea of what you think somebody else's idea of yourself should be." – *Henry David Thoreau*

Be yourself

You and I have distinct contributions to make to the promotion of God's glory. That is why we are here, so let's not waste our lives trying to be anything other than the masterpiece God has made us to be. This is very difficult. Tragically some people are born into families where from their earliest years they are given signals that they don't live up to expectations. "If only you were like your sister!" As we thought in chapter one, our society can place all kinds of expectations upon us, to have exactly the right body image, to succeed in this area or that; the list is endless. The church can get into this dangerous, damaging game as well. We present identikit pictures of spirituality. These pictures often inhibit personality, pressing us into a mould.

> Lift up your eyes! You are certainly a creature of time, but you are also a child of eternity. You are a citizen of heaven, and an alien and exile on earth, a pilgrim travelling to the celestial city. I read some years ago of a young man who found a five-dollar bill on the street and who 'from that time on never lifted his eyes

> when walking. In the course of years, he accumulated 29,516 buttons, 54,172 pins, 12 cents, a bent back and a miserly disposition.' But think what he lost. He could not see the radiance of the sunlight, the sheen of the stars, the smile on the face of his friends or the blossoms of springtime, for his eyes were in the gutter. There are too many Christians like that. We have important duties on earth, but we must never allow them to preoccupy us in such a way that we forget who we are and where we are going.[9]

Stereotyping

I was brought up in a Free Church. It was wonderful in many ways, but there was suspicion of anything liturgical, anything too emotional, and definitely anything charismatic. A "spiritual" person attended church regularly, listened well to the good Bible teaching, and was particularly regular in attendance at the communion service, which appeared to be a service of greater importance than the other services. Good Christians were "separate from the world". This was expressed in many ways. I had very little experience of the arts in my youth. Music, other than "Christian music", was not considered healthy, though some classical music passed the test. The cinema and the theatre were not places where the faithful believer would be found. I still remember the shock of being moved for the first time by liturgical worship, and of meeting a Christian West End actor and a Christian artist who spoke about "painting for the glory of God". We must resist spiritual stereotyping, and have confidence to

9 D. M. Howard (ed.), *Declare his Glory Among the Nations*, Downers Grove, IL: Inter-Varsity Press, 1977, page 90.

be ourselves before God and among His people. The kind of stereotyping mentioned above was much to do with the Christian culture of the day. I wonder what stereotypes the Christian culture of our day is manufacturing?

A beautiful tapestry

We are God's masterpiece as individuals, but when we are together in the church, we also manifest His skill. This masterpiece, which is His church, will be seen by cosmic powers as well as our fellow men and women. God's "intent was that now, through the church, the manifold wisdom of God should be made known to the rulers and authorities in the heavenly realms" (Ephesians 3:10). John Stott writes, "The church as a multi-racial, multi-cultural community is like a beautiful tapestry. Its members come from a wide range of colourful backgrounds. No other human community resembles it. Its diversity and harmony are unique. It is God's new society. And the many coloured fellowship of the church is a reflection of the many coloured (or 'many splendoured,' to use Francis Thompson's word) wisdom of God."[10]

The church should be a community of freedom where difference is celebrated but, as mentioned earlier, this can be far from the reality. The pressure to conform to a certain way of being can be considerable. This can sometimes be both sad and amusing. I remember one church that I went to where having a serene smile at all times seemed to be the essence of

---

10 John Stott, *God's New Society*, Downers Grove, IL: Inter-Varsity Press, page 123.

spirituality. I found this quite alarming, especially early on a Sunday morning. But the alarm turned to amusement when the flautist in the worship band sought to retain the smile while playing her flute!

Restoration required

I know only too well that this masterpiece has been soiled. The fall has marred the image of God in me, but it hasn't destroyed it. Restoration, indeed recreation, have taken place. The God who brought order and beauty out of primeval chaos (Genesis 1:2) has been doing it ever since in individual lives. We saw the contrast in chapter three of this book. I was "dead in [my] transgressions and sins" (Ephesians 2:1). Now I have been "made alive with Christ" (verse 5). I used to live in these sins (verse 2). Now there are good works which God has prepared in advance for me to do (verse 10).

Everything restored

We are part of a much larger canvas. God is renewing His soiled creation. This beautiful but broken world is on the edge of its seat: "The creation waits in eager expectation for the children of God to be revealed. For the creation was subjected to frustration, not by its own choice, but by the will of the one who subjected it, in hope that the creation itself will be liberated from its bondage to decay and brought into the freedom and glory of the children of God. We know that the whole creation has been groaning as in the pains of childbirth right up to the present time" (Romans 8:19–22). We are on the edge of our seat as well: "Not only so, but we ourselves, who have the firstfruits of the Spirit, groan inwardly as we wait eagerly for our adoption to sonship, the redemption of our bodies" (verse 23).

J. B. Phillips in his paraphrase depicts us as "standing on tiptoe" to see the children of God being revealed. When we are finally seen to be the children of God, our true identity finally revealed, and the glory that awaits us is finally ours, this will turn the key in the lock and the renewal of the whole of creation will take place. Ever since the fall, creation has been under the judgment of God, and consequently, as our experience tells us, has been in "bondage to decay". Nature is breathtakingly beautiful, but at the same time capable of the most gruesome horrors. As we have recognized, humankind is capable of the most heroic, apparently selfless, sacrifice and yet in the next moment the most dreadful selfishness.

But this won't be forever. What God is doing in us, as He transforms us into the image of His Son, is part of something much bigger: the redemption and renewal of creation.

CHAPTER EIGHT

Jesus and Identity

Secure in His identity

If ever there was someone who was completely comfortable with his own identity, it was Jesus. Though He lived with bold conviction of His identity, He was interested to know what others thought. "Who do people say the Son of Man is?" (Matthew 16:13). There was confusion in the response: "Some say one thing, some another" (verse 14, paraphrased). Actually in their confusion they probably felt they were paying Him the highest of compliments. "Some say John the Baptist; others say Elijah; and still others, Jeremiah or one of the prophets." All three, for different reasons, were considered to be among the greatest of men in Israel's history. Jesus personalizes His question: "'But what about you?' he asked. 'Who do you say I am?' Simon Peter answered, 'You are the Christ, the Son of the living God'" (verses 15–16). There may have been confusion among the people, but there is total certainty with Jesus. His immediate response to Peter is, "'Blessed are you, Simon son of Jonah, for this was not revealed to you by man, but by my Father in heaven'" (verse 17). He knew who He was; it was His Father in heaven who was revealing the truth about Him to His disciples.

The way Jesus dealt with others shows both His acceptance of their true identity, and His comfort with His own. If you were a woman, a slave, or living in poverty at the time of Christ, you were considered virtually a non-person. The respect with which Jesus dealt with the woman at the well (John 4), the woman taken in adultery (John 8:1–11), the prostitute at the meal hosted by Simon the Pharisee (Luke 7:36–50), the demon-possessed man known as Legion (Luke 8:26–39), and Zacchaeus the tax collector (Luke 19:1–10) shows clearly that Jesus saw them as made in the image of God. There are many other examples – including the way He treated children – which surprised onlookers and His disciples alike.

He was not concerned by what others might think of Him for treating any of these groups or individuals in this way. For Simon the Pharisee, it was reason enough to come to a conclusion about Jesus. "If this man were a prophet, he would know... what kind of woman she is – that she is a sinner" (Luke 7:39). Jesus asks Simon, "Do you see this woman?" (verse 44). He clearly didn't. He only saw her as she had been, a prostitute, and probably thought, once a prostitute always a prostitute: a leopard can't change its spots. He did not see what she had become, a woman clearly devoted to Jesus. Jesus treated her as He treated everybody, as a person of value – and He treated people like that before they came to faith, as well as afterwards.

When Jesus met with the woman at the well, we find that the disciples "were surprised" (the word denotes incredulous surprise)[11] "to find him talking with a woman" (John 4:27). They would have been more surprised if they had known what kind of woman she was. She had already had five husbands and the man she was living with at the time was not her husband (John 4:17). Bruce Milne comments, "Through the entire conversation Jesus deals with her as a person in her own right, with her unique history and special longings. She emerges in the account as a credible character with personal dignity – because Jesus treats her as such. Simply put, Jesus loved her and was prepared to breach age-old conventions to reach her… The disciples' astonishment at Jesus conversing with the woman reflects their conformity to the sexual prejudices of their society; risking the scandal involved in speaking with a woman, especially one like this, was simply not to be tolerated."[12]

Identity challenged

Read Matthew 3:13 – 4:11.

At the beginning of His public ministry, Jesus came to the River Jordan to be baptized by John the Baptist. As soon as He was baptized (Matthew 3:16), there was a dramatic affirmation of His identity. Heaven opened, the Spirit of God

11 Leon Morris, *New International Commentary on the New Testament*, Grand Rapids, MI: Eerdmans, 1971.
12 Bruce Milne, *The Message of John*, Downers Grove, IL: Inter-Varsity Press, 1993, page 86.

visibly descended in the form of a dove, lighting on Jesus, and the divine voice spoke, "This is my Son, whom I love; with him I am well pleased" (verse 17). What comfort it must have brought to Jesus, knowing the many challenges ahead, to have this dramatic affirmation.

Satan knows the power of such certainty. "Then Jesus was led by the Spirit into the desert to be tempted by the devil" (Matthew 4:1). This intensive time of temptation followed immediately after the affirmation of His baptism, and the temptations were all about His identity. Look at the contrasts: "A voice from heaven said, 'This is my Son'" (3:17). Then the voice of Satan said, "If you are the Son of God" (4:3). It was a deliberate attempt to destroy Jesus' absolute assurance of His identity. Satan seemed to have a strong argument. "The Son of God is hungry? What nonsense! Does not your Father have the power to provide for you even in a barren wilderness?" The answer Jesus gives confirms His absolute assurance of His identity. "Jesus answered, 'It is written: "Man does not live on bread alone, but on every word that comes from the mouth of God"'' (verse 4). In other words: "There is something more important than bread for the sustaining of life and that is the creative, energizing power of My Father to sustain Me and I have no doubt of His paternal care."

Satan doesn't give up without a fight. "If you say you are so sure of your identity, prove it" – that is his next tactic. "Then the devil took him to the holy city and had him stand on the highest point of the temple. 'If you are the Son of God,' he said, 'throw yourself down'" (4:5–6). He even quotes Scripture to make his point (verse 6 – paraphrased): "If you are so sure of your identity as the Son of God, then no doubt you can be sure of His protection, so let's have a demonstration of that." It's a powerful temptation. We all like the opportunity to prove the truth of a point we have made. Also, after thirty years of anonymity, Satan is saying to Jesus, "Go out there and make a name for yourself. Get yourself a reputation."

But getting a reputation was never on Jesus' "to do" list. In fact, when He healed people, He often asked them to keep it a secret (not that it seems anyone took much notice of this secrecy). When He finally was welcomed into the city with palms strewn before Him, it made no difference to Him. And a week later, when He stood before the Jewish leaders and then before Pilate, He was not worried about what people thought of Him. He knew who He was, what He had been called to do, and whom He was serving.

He has no need to make a name for Himself because it is impossible to add to the title "Son of God"!

Satan still hasn't given up! "Again, the devil took him to a very high mountain and showed him all the kingdoms of the world and their splendour. 'All this I will give you,' he said, 'if you will bow down and worship me'" (verses 8–9). Jesus is at the beginning of His public ministry. He has a road to tread which has been mapped out by His Father. He knows that road leads to a cross. He also knows that, without the cross, He cannot obtain the crown, but now there is a suggestion of an easier road, an immediate kingdom. But the insidious suggestion is immediately resisted. His father, who has called Him, will sustain Him, and in that Jesus happily rests.

Freed to serve

At His baptism, the response of John the Baptist is hardly surprising: "I need to be baptized by you, and do you come to me?" This is all the wrong way round! But when you are secure in your identity, you are ready to take a seemingly lowly place. Here Jesus the eternal Son of God identifies Himself with us and with our need; this identification will reach its climax at the cross.

Not only is Jesus ready to identify Himself with fallen humanity, He is ready to serve fallen humanity. Jesus knows the end cannot be far off. "Jesus knew that the time (hour) had come for him to leave this world and go to the Father" (John 13:1). As He is having a meal with His disciples, a situation arises which Jesus grasps and uses as a tool for teaching. Guests arriving in a home after a journey on the dusty roads expected to have their feet washed by a slave in the house. It was a task considered to be so humble, no Jewish slave would ever be required to perform it, but apparently there was no slave present at this meal. Maybe Jesus had deliberately arranged it that way. None of the disciples are prepared to do the slave's work. You do not wash the feet of your peers! In the other three Gospel accounts of this evening, we are told that a dispute broke out among the disciples over which of them would be the greatest in Christ's coming kingdom.

It was when the evening meal was being served (verse 2) that Jesus "took off his outer clothing, and wrapped a towel round his waist" and began to wash the feet of His disciples (verses 4–5). What the disciples are unwilling to do for each other, the Son of God is ready to do for all of them. The fact that Jesus is doing this when the meal is already being served, and they are already reclining on their couches, shows that this is something more than the usual act of courtesy. It is a "parable in action setting out the great principle of lowly service".[13] (It was also, of course, as Jesus would go on to explain to Peter, symbolic of the cleansing which Jesus would procure for His people through the greatest act of lowly service in dying at Calvary.

Where does the freedom which allows such acts of selfless service come from? Where does the resistance to such acts of selfless service come from? It is all to do with identity. The disciples that night were concerned with position, status, and reputation. These concerns lead to the need to be served and the battle to ensure that no one usurps your place.

Where does the freedom to serve come from? When you know who you are, and you know that status is secure, then you are able to give yourself freely in service to God and to others. "Jesus knew that the Father had put all things under his power, and that he had come from God and was returning to God; so..." (verse 3). That word "so" is vital here – the assurance leads to the actions. Jesus is secure in His identity, His calling, present and future.

As Jesus serves the disciples at the meal, as He goes to the cross in service to all of us, He does not lose sight for a moment of His eternal status: "Christ Jesus: who, being in very nature God, did not consider equality with

---

13 Leon Morris, *New International Commentary on the New Testament*, Grand Rapids, MI: Eerdmans, 1971, page 612.

God something to be grasped, but made himself nothing, taking the very nature of a servant, being made in human likeness" (Philippians 2:5–7). From the moment of our birth as we cry until we are fed the focus is on us – our needs, our desires. Jesus had access to privileges and power beyond our understanding but He freely gave them up. His focus was on His Father's will, His Father's glory, rather than His own needs and desires. He "made himself nothing". He "humbled himself". But He did not leave this with us as an example to admire. He left it as a challenge to emulate: "Your attitude should be the same as that of Christ Jesus."

Do you see the difference we could make in the world, if we accept who we are in Christ? Then we can serve, rather than always looking to be served. Then we can take the lowly place, do the menial task joyfully. We now know we have nothing to prove, and therefore no need for all our acts of service to be noted by others. It is life- and world-changing to know who you are in Christ.

CHAPTER NINE

A New Creation

Read Romans 6:1–14:

> *What shall we say, then? Shall we go on sinning, so that grace may increase? By no means! We are those who have died to sin; how can we live in it any longer? Or don't you know that all of us who were baptized into Christ Jesus were baptized into his death? We were therefore buried with him through baptism into death in order that, just as Christ was raised from the dead through the glory of the Father, we too may live a new life.*
>
> *For if we have been united with him in a death like his, we will certainly also be united with him in a resurrection like his. For we know that our old self was crucified with him so that the body ruled by sin might be done away with, that we should no longer be slaves to sin – because anyone who has died has been set free from sin.*
>
> *Now if we died with Christ, we believe that we will also live with him. For we know that since Christ*

was raised from the dead, he cannot die again; death no longer has mastery over him. The death he died, he died to sin once for all; but the life he lives, he lives to God.

In the same way, count yourselves dead to sin but alive to God in Christ Jesus. Therefore do not let sin reign in your mortal body so that you obey its evil desires. Do not offer any part of yourself to sin as an instrument of wickedness, but rather offer yourselves to God as those who have been brought from death to life; and offer every part of yourself to him as an instrument of righteousness. For sin shall no longer be your master, because you are not under the law, but under grace.

The old has gone forever

Oscar Pistorius, a South African and indeed global hero, the first disabled athlete to compete in the Olympic Games, was convicted first of culpable homicide, then later, on appeal, convicted of the murder of his girlfriend Reeva Steenkamp. His biographer said that, "Pistorius had convinced himself he would find no other woman who combined the worldly attributes he sought with a habit of Sunday church going and praying together, heads bowed and hands entwined, before every meal. It had not just been about her beauty, he had convinced himself, nor a mere exercise in shoring up his frail vanity. They were bonded by mutual affection and the pursuit of glamour, money, luxury cars, sex and – simultaneously –

Christ's redemptive love" (from *The Sunday Times* extract from *Chase Your Shadow: The Trials of Oscar Pistorius* by John Carlin, 2014, Atlantic Books).

Jesus spoke of being born again. Following Him is not an addition to life as you are now living it. That is how some people appear to view their commitment to the Christian faith, and it does not seem to alter their lives to any great degree. Everything goes on very much as it did before, with a few nice additions, particularly on a Sunday morning! Paul wrote to the church in Corinth, "If anyone is in Christ, the new creation has come; the old has gone, the new has come!" (2 Corinthians 5:17). It is interesting that Paul uses here the language of creation. The person who is not a Christian, just like Paul had been, is living in darkness. The earth was in darkness until God said, "Let there be light," and immediately light filled the earth, dispelling the darkness. He now gives life and light to those who are spiritually dead and in darkness. But this is no small thing. This is no minor addition. It's from death to life, from darkness to light.

Isn't it fabulous that "the old has gone"? Take a moment just to reflect on that. If you are struggling with shame about past sinful failure, ask God for the faith to believe this truth. The old has gone. It is gone because it has been dealt with. All the guilt and shame of those failures are gone. It has been removed as far as the east is from the west (Psalm 103:12). Think about it: that is a long way, an incalculable distance. It has been removed so far that no trace of it can ever be found. It is God's work to do this. As in all of the work which God accomplishes, He has done this perfectly. Jesus has borne our sins so far away that Satan can never actually bring them back. That sin, however much the memory of it may torment you, can never hurt you again.

> It is encouraging to do a little Bible study, to discover what God has done with our sin.
>
> "Surely it was for my benefit that I suffered such anguish. In your love you kept me from the pit of destruction; you have put all my sins behind your back" (Isaiah 38:17).
>
> "Come now, let us settle the matter," says the Lord. "Though your sins are like scarlet, they shall be as white as snow; though they are red as crimson, they shall be like wool" (Isaiah 1:18).
>
> "When you were dead in your sins and in the uncircumcision of your flesh, God made you alive with Christ. He forgave us all our sins, having cancelled the charge of our legal indebtedness, which stood against us and condemned us; he has taken it away, nailing it to the cross" (Colossians 2:13–14).

We can live a new life today because death has taken place. Paul writes, "Just as Christ was raised from the dead through the glory of the Father, we too may live a new life" (Romans 6:4). He is using the illustration of baptism. We were united with Christ as he bore sin's penalty at the cross. As we go under the water of baptism, it is a vivid and deeply moving symbol of our identification with Christ in His death. Jesus paid the penalty once and for all, and we were completely identified with Him. Sin has no claim on Christ. He has dealt with it. We were identified with Him, as He dealt with sin. It has no further claim on us. It cannot come back and bite us. What was true of Christ is true of us.

The slate is clean

I remember the day a very close friend of mine, who had got into trouble with the law, fulfilled the sentence which had been imposed by the court. Up until that point, at any moment the police could call him in or call on him unannounced. He was living in constant uncertainty. Then the day came when he completed his sentence. The prescribed price for his crime was fully paid. He was a free man again. That was a great moment. It was an unforgettable day for me, and I was only his friend. The day of our salvation was an even greater day. My friend will have a record of his wrong for the rest of his life. That will never be forgotten. It's on his record. As far as my past wrongs are concerned, the price has been fully paid, and the record has been cleared. When the chief prosecutor approaches God with his arguments, asking for my previous record to be taken into account, it's found to be clean. There is no sign of even a blemish!

Are you beginning to get the idea of what it means to be "a new creation"? The old life of sin is finished, and we have died to it. The totally new life of the justified sinner has begun. Everything is new. Our past has been dealt with, and the future is dramatically transformed. New desires, ambitions, and goals will dominate our lives.

Plain sailing?

And we all lived happily ever after! Not quite. We need to constantly remind ourselves of our new identity. Although, as I have said, I became a follower of Jesus when very young, I didn't stay that way in my teenage years. Other things seemed too attractive! So I backslid for a while. Sheer common sense brought me back to faith.

Paul continues in Romans 6:11, "in the same way, count yourselves dead to sin but alive to God in Christ Jesus." I want nothing more to do with my old life. It is dead and buried. I want nothing more to do with the sin and the shame of that old life. I want nothing more to do with its slavery, even though that slavery sometimes presented itself as freedom. So I need to constantly remind myself who I am. I am a new man in Christ. It is not a case of, "If I tell myself often enough, something might happen to me." This is the reality. I need to constantly remind myself because the world, the flesh, and the devil are constantly trying to convince me otherwise. A major secret of Christian discipleship is simply believing the truth about you. Say "No" to the enemy's suggestions, and "Yes" to the truth about you, as God has revealed it in His word and constantly confirms it by His Spirit.

The verses which follow are so liberating: "Therefore do not let sin reign in your mortal body so that you obey its evil desires. Do not offer any part of yourself to sin as an instrument of wickedness, but rather offer yourselves to God as those who have been brought from death to life; and offer every part of yourself to him as an instrument of righteousness. For sin shall not be your master, because you are not under the law, but under grace" (Romans 6:12–14).

It is liberating because now, in Christ, it is possible. "Sin shall not be your master." We used to be under its control. It mastered us. But no longer; the redemption price has been paid and we are free from its tyranny, as we saw in chapter four: we are no longer slaves but children and heirs.

The choice is now yours

Sin hasn't given up the fight, however. Now that we are free, we must remain free. We are now free to fight against it. This is spiritual warfare; this is the daily joy and discipline of discipleship.

Paul gives some very specific instructions. Firstly, "Do not let sin reign in your mortal body" (verse 12). You see it wants to take back control. It wants to say to you, "You are nothing but a wretched sinner, you can never be any different, and you are powerless to change." That is a lie. Yes, you and I are wretched sinners, but that no longer says everything about us, or even the most important thing. Christ has accepted us, dealt with that wretched sin, paid its full penalty, and delivered us from its consequences and its power. I am a child of God, and He reigns in my life by His Spirit. Sin has no place here. Sadly I still sin, but now sin is an enemy intrusion. It is not something I embrace, it is something I hate. I will never let it reign. I will deal with it immediately, in confession and repentance. It will never again dominate my life, or be my identity definer.

Secondly, Paul makes specific mention here of the mortal body and then goes on to write, "Do not offer any part of yourself to sin as an instrument of wickedness" (Romans 6:13). We have a choice. We can offer the various parts of our body to God for His glory and service or we can use the parts of our body for ourselves to serve the purposes of evil. My hand can be used to kill or to heal. My lips can be used to bless or to curse. My brain can be used to build an empire for me to serve myself or to make a contribution to the ever-expanding kingdom of my Lord. The Holy Spirit is there, urging and empowering me to make the right choices. But the enemy is never far away, making counter-suggestions and holding out false attractions. To whom am I going to yield today? To whom will I make my offering?

Because of the work of Christ, the choice is now mine. I am no longer a slave; I am a free man with the ability and the right to choose. I have the capacity to make the right choice, because the Holy Spirit is within me, giving me all the strength that I could ever require. Think of Paul. He had used his remarkable brain for things that were for his profit (Philippians 3:7). He had used his hands to take Christians into imprisonment. He had used his mouth to breathe out "murderous threats" against them (Acts 9:1). But now, by the power of the Holy Spirit within him, he was making different choices. He was committed, as he used his brain to write and preach and counsel and advise, to seeing God glorified. His hands were used to bless others, and to make tents to provide for his needs. This meant he would not be a burden to others, but be able to serve them. His lips were used to worship God, and to proclaim His truth and His love.

How we need God's help to consistently make the right choices. Here is Peter: one moment his lips are being used to express the truth about Jesus and for that he receives Christ's commendation. "'But what about you?' he asked, 'Who do you say I am?' Simon Peter answered, 'You are the Christ, the Son of the living God.' Jesus replied, 'Blessed are you, Simon son of Jonah, for this was not revealed to you by man, but by my Father in heaven'" (Matthew 16:15–17). But those same lips will be used to deny that he knew Jesus or was one of His disciples. "After a little while, those standing near said to Peter, 'Surely you are one of them, for you are a Galilean.' He began to call down curses on himself, and he swore to them, 'I don't know this man you're talking about'" (Mark 14:70–71). James is very clear on how our mouths can be used for worship or for wickedness. "With the tongue we praise our Lord and Father, and with it we curse human beings, who have been made in God's likeness" (James 3:9).

One of the most powerful testimonies I have come across lately is of a young man, Anthony Gielty, who was put in prison for a savage attack in which he used a samurai sword on another man. When he was a child, he had fallen in love with Jesus, but had then turned his back on Him, and invested in a life of violence and crime. Aged only seventeen, Anthony was so uncontrollable in prison that even the staff were wary of him, and it looked as though he would be sent on what is called the Ghost Train. This is a system used in prisons, where inmates who are out of control are kept in constant solitary confinement, and moved every few months, disorientating them further. It is a soul-destroying tactic, only used as a last resort. But then Anthony again met with Jesus and began to turn his life around. Tempted to go back to his old ways, God convicted him so deeply that he spent three days fasting, and he was totally transformed.[14]

This is our new and true identity: we are sons and daughters of God. We are no longer slaves to sin. It need master us no longer. The Holy Spirit within us enables us to use our freedom to make God-glorifying choices, choices which will establish and maintain our freedom.

---

14 Anthony's story is told in full in his book *Out of the Darkness*, published by Monarch Books

CHAPTER TEN

Extravagant Love

Read Luke 8:26–39:

> *They sailed to the region of the Gerasenes, which is across the lake from Galilee. When Jesus stepped ashore, he was met by a demon-possessed man from the town. For a long time this man had not worn clothes or lived in a house, but had lived in the tombs. When he saw Jesus, he cried out and fell at his feet, shouting at the top of his voice, "What do you want with me, Jesus, Son of the Most High God? I beg you, don't torture me!" For Jesus had commanded the impure spirit to come out of the man. Many times it had seized him, and though he was chained hand and foot and kept under guard, he had broken his chains and had been driven by the demon into solitary places.*
>
> *Jesus asked him, "What is your name?"*
>
> *"Legion," he replied, because many demons had gone into him. And they begged Jesus repeatedly not to order them to go into the Abyss.*

A large herd of pigs was feeding there on the hillside. The demons begged Jesus to let them go into the pigs, and he gave them permission. When the demons came out of the man, they went into the pigs, and the herd rushed down the steep bank into the lake and was drowned.

When those tending the pigs saw what had happened, they ran off and reported this in the town and countryside, and the people went out to see what had happened. When they came to Jesus, they found the man from whom the demons had gone out, sitting at Jesus' feet, dressed and in his right mind; and they were afraid. Those who had seen it told the people how the demon-possessed man had been cured. Then all the people of the region of the Gerasenes asked Jesus to leave them, because they were overcome with fear. So he got into the boat and left.

The man from whom the demons had gone out begged to go with him, but Jesus sent him away, saying, "Return home and tell how much God has done for you." So the man went away and told all over the town how much Jesus had done for him.

Dignity restored

He was possessed by a demon, uncontrollable, and self-destructive. He had become a walking example of the bondage that sin can bring to a human being. He was made in the image of God, created by God, and placed in a position of control within His creation, as we all have been. God's command was, "Be fruitful and increase in number; fill the earth and subdue it. Rule over the fish of the sea and the birds of the air and over every living creature that moves on the ground" (Genesis 1:28). God made us to rule, not be ruled. He made us to be free, not bound. He gave us a position of dignity within His creation. But this man was now the very opposite of what he was created to be. He was under the control of demons, not in a place of control. He was bound, not free. The description of him, physically chained and being guarded in the tombs, illustrates his desperate state. He appeared to have lost all dignity. "For a long time he had not worn clothes or lived in a house" (Luke 8:27). He had been driven by the demons into solitary places (verse 29). God made us so that we would thrive in community. Satan is forever separating. He separates us from God, and from one another.

See now the incredible power of redemption. Jesus dealt with the demons in the man, and they entered a herd of pigs. This led to the destruction of the pigs which must have caused quite a stir. So the people came out to see what had happened. I am sure they were astonished when they found the demon-possessed man sitting at the feet of Jesus, dressed and in his right mind. It's a brilliant picture of peace restored. This man had been uncontrollable. He could not control himself and others could not control him. The chain which it was hoped would restrain him was broken by the power of the demons within him, and then he was driven by the spirits where he did not want to go. But now he was sitting at the feet of Jesus at peace. He was dressed, and in his right mind. I wonder how long it had been since he could sit untroubled, free and feeling human?

Jesus is in the business of restoring dignity to those who are made in the image of God. Sin has marred that image, but in Christ it is restored. Paul writes in Ephesians 4:22–24, "You were taught, with regard to your former way of life, to put off your old self, which is being corrupted by its deceitful desires; to be made new in the attitude of your minds; and to put on the new self, created to be like God in true righteousness and holiness." At the moment of my conversion, I "put off my old self".

When I come in from a run, and it has been very wet, I will be covered in mud. And then I will want to get my dirty clothes off immediately, and to put on new clean ones. My old self is just like those dirty clothes. There is one difference though: the old nature is "*being* corrupted by its deceitful desires". The longer I leave it on, the dirtier it becomes! My putting off of the old nature and my putting on of "the new self, created to be like God in true righteousness and holiness", is a decisive, once and for all act, which by the power of the Holy Spirit takes place at my conversion. This decisive act leads to a continuous process. Now, writes Paul, you need "to be made new in the attitude of your minds". A daily continuous renewal of our minds, and our whole outlook on life, will take place as we respond to the work of the Holy Spirit now at work within us. Having been made new, my life must begin again in Christ, in the Spirit's power, as a whole new way of thinking and living opens up for me.

The thrilling end result of this is that this new self is "created to be like God". Increasingly, as we cooperate with the Holy Spirit at work in us, He is able to produce His holy character, with the amazing prospect that one day we will be presented "before his glorious presence without fault and with great joy" (Jude 24).

The gift of God

So the work of Christ in our lives by His Spirit gives more than forgiveness, truly wonderful though that is. It is the work of regeneration. It is to be born again, to receive new life. The demon-possessed man was not just forgiven the wrongs he had done, he was redeemed from "his former way of life". Now he could "put off" his "old self", and put on "the new self, created to be like God in true righteousness and holiness". The power to do this was the power of the Holy Spirit now within him. The fact never to be forgotten about the Holy Spirit is that He is given to glorify Christ (John 16:14). Now the demon-possessed man, and every follower of Christ, has power within to live a life which glorifies Christ rather than a life which pleases self and destroys self. "Supernatural living through supernatural empowering is at the very heart of New Testament Christianity."[15]

Jesus was very clear as He prepared to leave His disciples. "I will not leave you as orphans; I will come to you" (John 14:18). Three days after His death He came dramatically

15 J. I. Packer, *Keep in Step with the Spirit*, Downers Grove, IL: Inter-Varsity Press, 2005, page 24.

to them. His ascension after forty days did not leave them bereft: "I will ask the Father, and he will give you another counsellor to be with you for ever – the Spirit of truth" (John 14:16–17). The word translated "counsellor" is *Paraclete*. It is a tough word to translate. As well as "counsellor" it could be translated "helper" or "advocate" or "comforter". It literally means "someone who comes alongside to help". Notice Jesus says the Father will give you "another" counsellor. Jesus had been alongside His disciples as their counsellor and friend and now the Father would send the Holy Spirit to carry on that "alongside" ministry. Jesus in fact continues His alongside ministry through the Holy Spirit within us.

As the disciples watched Jesus being betrayed, convicted, and crucified, they lost all hope and confidence. The sad words to the stranger who came alongside the two disciples walking towards Emmaus summed up their mood: "we had hoped that he was the one who was going to redeem Israel" (Luke 24:21). Hope was a thing of the past. The disciples were behind locked doors for fear of the Jews (John 20:19). Who were they now? They had been disciples of an increasingly famous teacher, but what now?

The change as you watch and listen to them in the Acts of the Apostles could not be clearer. They know the risen Jesus is with them by His Spirit. Their boldness, their confidence are clear. No intimidation or persecution can silence them – not even the threat of death will stop them. They know who they are, and they know what they have to do.

Do you know who you are? You are a child of God; Jesus walks alongside you by His Spirit. He is the Spirit of truth and power. He is the Holy Spirit constantly seeking to glorify Christ in and through you, constantly calling and empowering you to live a holy life.

Extravagant love

God's desire and purpose is that we should, as His children, be living in freedom and with purpose, but for some, their lives resemble more the isolation and the bondage of the man who lived in the tombs. We need to trust the word of God about us. "How great is the love the Father has lavished on us, that we should be called children of God! And that is what we are!" (1 John 3:1).

Do you really believe you are lavishly loved by God? The word "lavish" conveys the idea of extravagance. One speaker I heard referred to the "wastefully abundant" love of God for us. This is always something I struggle with. As I mentioned earlier I was brought up in a wonderful Christian home, but it was also what I would call a very careful home. There was nothing much to spare at the end of the week when all the bills had been paid. My parents rarely invested in anything just for them to enjoy. This has certainly impacted on me. I find it quite difficult to spend anything on myself, certainly on anything that I don't actually need. It has been even more the case with time. Spending time, just for me to relax and enjoy, has been a huge challenge. God had time for a Sabbath, I rarely did! I don't do extravagance. It has been difficult for me to appreciate the extravagant love of God for me, and to live in the good of that. But sons and daughters can relax in their own home. They don't need to "do" to be accepted; they just need to be who they are – sons and daughters.

It has been difficult for me to grasp the lavish love of God though I was brought up in an atmosphere of love and care. How much more difficult it will be, if in your formative years you have known nothing of such love. A loving spouse, and the love and care of friends can help to heal the damage you have experienced, but such damage is often deep and long-lasting. Establishing a true view of who you are now in Christ, and experiencing the lavish love of God may be a gradual progressive experience, and you may need help from others on the journey. Whatever you have been told by others, whatever you may feel about yourself, God's word declares your adoption into a family where the family head knows only lavish love for all His children.

That is who we are, so let's relax in the Father's extravagant love.

CHAPTER ELEVEN

Let the Journey Begin

The foundation for growth

Imagine a top athlete, preparing for the next Olympics, who is uncertain whether he will quite make it into the British Olympics team. He is training as hard as he can, trying to balance his job, his family, and his training. Then he gets the email saying he is in. The relief will be enormous, and things will get even better when he is informed that he has also qualified for special funding. He will be able to leave his job, concentrate full-time on training, and soon his racing times will improve. With the uncertainties behind him, he will be able to focus on the task in hand.

I hope for you that uncertainties regarding your position in Christ, uncertainties with regard to the Father's love for you, are over. Now you can relax and focus on the task, and the joy of every Christian, of growing in your knowledge of Christ and developing your walk with Him.

Once we have accepted who we are in Christ, we can

begin to dream of what God wants us to become. As we dream we have the absolute cast-iron assurance of what we will one day be. As we saw in the previous chapter, we *will* be presented "before his glorious presence without fault and with great joy" (Jude 24). The transformation will be total. Even our bodies will be changed. "And just as we have borne the likeness of the earthly man, so shall we bear the likeness of the man from heaven" (1 Corinthians 15:49). In heaven our learning and developing will continue. Jesus said, "Now this is eternal life: that they may know you, the only true God, and Jesus Christ, whom you have sent" (John 17:3). Don Carson says that, "Eternal life is not so much everlasting life as knowledge of the everlasting one".[16] When we receive eternal life in Christ, we joyfully rest in His finished work, but we also take the first step on a long and wonderful journey of discovery.

Resting and running

We rest, and yet we are to walk with Christ; we run the race, we fight the fight. The Christian life from beginning to end is constant movement. High on an alpine mountain, etched into the rock face, is the name of a climber. Underneath the date of his death is the simple epitaph, "He died climbing." The progress we make is rarely, if ever, depicted by a smooth constantly rising line on a graph. It is more like a jagged rock face. So many ups and downs, and yet progress is being made, however erratically transformation is taking place:

---

16 Don Carson, *The Gospel According to John*, Downers Grove, IL: Inter-Varsity Press, 1991.

"We, who with unveiled faces all reflect the Lord's glory, are being transformed into his likeness with ever-increasing glory" (2 Corinthians 3:18).

I remember when John Stott came to the Keswick Convention to preach for the last time. He was not well, and looked frail as he stood up to preach. But as soon as he started to speak, all that was forgotten as he said, "I want to share with you where my mind has come to rest as I approach the end of my pilgrimage on earth and it is – God wants his people to become like Christ. Christlikeness is the will of God for the people of God."

The destination of our journey is Christlikeness. We are being transformed into His likeness. It is happening now! Your reading of this book can be part of this progressive process. This is what the Christian life is all about. "For those God foreknew he also predestined to be conformed to the image of his Son" (Romans 8:29). God's eternal purpose is that His chosen people should become like Jesus. We can do many things for Christ, but if in the doing of those things, we are not becoming more like Christ, we have missed the primary purpose of the Christian life. In my life, I have had times when things have got completely out of balance. Extreme busyness in "Christian service" has left no time to develop my walk with Christ and left me irritable through weariness. This is hardly what developing in Christlikeness is supposed to resemble.

> William Temple, Archbishop of Canterbury in the 1940s, once said, "It is no good giving me a play like

> Hamlet or King Lear and telling me to write a play like that. Shakespeare could do it – I can't. And it is no good showing me a life like the life of Jesus and telling me to live a life like that. Jesus could do it – I can't. But if the genius of Shakespeare could come and live in me, then I could write plays like his. And if the Spirit could come into me, then I could live a life like His."

The running partner

We have a companion on every step of this journey. As we have recognized, God the Holy Spirit no longer lives in man-made temples. He inhabits us individually and as the Christian community. He is God's great gift to us, and His presence gives us the assurance I have been urging us to embrace as our rightful inheritance, "because those who are led by the Spirit of God are the sons of God. For you did not receive a spirit that makes you a slave again to fear, but you received the Spirit of sonship. And by him we cry, '*Abba*, Father.' The Spirit himself testifies with our spirit that we are God's children" (Romans 8:14–16).

His presence is wonderfully comforting, but constantly challenging. He is the Holy Spirit, and He constantly calls us to grow in holiness. He works for change at the very depths of our being, subduing and resisting the drive of the flesh, transforming us to be like Christ. I am heading towards a meeting as I write this. I believe a decision needs to be taken at this meeting which will impact on me. It means I will lose the opportunity to be involved in something that I have really enjoyed for many years. If I say nothing, then there will be no change. That is what my flesh wants. But I know what is right, and there is no doubt in my mind that the Holy Spirit within me is urging me to do the right thing. It is a battle, but I know that on this issue, as with so many other issues in life, saying "Yes" to the Holy Spirit and "No" to the drive of the flesh is ultimately going to make me more like Christ. And that is what the Christian life is all about.

It's the fruit of the Holy Spirit

Read Galatians 5:16–25.

So our life attitude must be repudiation of the flesh and total surrender to the Holy Spirit. Gradually we will see the fruit of this in our lives. It is what Paul calls "the fruit of the Spirit". "The fruit of the Spirit is love, joy, peace, patience, kindness, goodness, faithfulness, gentleness and self-control" (Galatians 5:22–23). As you read those characteristics, whom do you think of? I think of Jesus. It is a portrait of Christ. As we cooperate with the Holy Spirit at work within us, the fruit will be growth in Christlikeness. John Stott helpfully points out that these "nine Christian graces seem to portray a Christian's attitude to God, to other people and to himself."[17] The change which the Holy Spirit is bringing touches and transforms every area of our lives. Love, joy, and peace show what our attitude towards God should be. One of my main reasons for writing this book is that we might

17 John Stott, *The Message of Galatians*, Downers Grove, IL: Inter-Varsity Press, 1968, page 148.

get to that place where "peace" is the word we would use to describe our relationship with God. Resting in our complete acceptance in Christ, our greatest joy is to know God and to have this brilliant privilege of walking with Him. As we understand more of who He is, a continuing transformation takes place, and Christlikeness is progressively seen. Our first love becomes our love for Him. It is this primary love which influences our decisions and our choices. A love relationship is the essence of Christian discipleship. It is the soil in which true holiness grows, not through legalistic rule-keeping, but through decisions motivated by love.

How we treat others is so dependent on our view of ourselves. "Let us not become conceited, provoking and envying each other" (Galatians 5:26). "We will not compare ourselves with each other as if one of us were better and another worse. We have far more interesting things to do with our lives. Each of us is an original" (Galatians 5:26, *The Message*). If we fail to see ourselves as God's masterpiece, fallen but redeemed and now totally accepted as His sons and daughters, the danger is our human relationships will quickly become competitive. Needing to prove ourselves, the twin dangers are "provoking and envying". We will challenge people because we need to prove our superiority to ourselves and show it to others. Alternatively, we will go into our shells, because we are envious of someone's personality or abilities. Even worse, we may begin to actively plan to somehow bring that person down.

When we are keeping in step with the Spirit (verse 25), the fruit which will impact on our relationships is seen not in competition but in our patience, kindness, and goodness. "Longsuffering" is one of the most beautiful words to describe how we should relate to one another. God has certainly been longsuffering with me. I disappoint myself so often as I realize that I have to learn the lessons God teaches me over and over again. If I disappoint myself, you can imagine how the heart of God must be saddened. But God is so patient, so longsuffering. Consider the patience of Jesus with His outspoken but failing, denying disciple Peter. Jesus deals so graciously and patiently with him that he develops to become one of the most significant influences in the early church, and he is still influencing the church through his writings today.

The way God deals with me is the example of how I should deal with others. Kindness must be my heart attitude. I can be kind because I don't need to be constantly looking for things for me in this relationship. I know, and have accepted, who I am in Christ: now I am able to give myself to others. If you know your worth in Christ, if His acceptance of you is the basis of your self-esteem, and if you are convinced that it is in Christ that everyone's true identity is found, then you are free to love others selflessly. No more competition, the constant need to get one up on someone else. No more constant navel-gazing, always worried that you don't quite match up. You are no longer desperately craving for acceptance in your relationships but serving and giving yourself to others.

This kindness will lead to goodness in our actions and words. Goodness is essential to our witness. Peter, as he writes the letter we know as First Peter, is teaching the believers how they are to live in a world which opposes them. Have a quick read through the letter and see how Peter emphasizes that we must live good lives. "Live such good lives among the pagans that, though they accuse you of doing wrong, they may see your good deeds and glorify God on the day he visits us" (1 Peter 2:12). "For it is God's will that by doing good you should silence the ignorant talk of foolish people" (verse 15). How I treat my brother or sister, particularly when they let me down, and how I live in the world are essential aspects of my witness.

So how should we treat ourselves? "Faithfulness, gentleness and self-control" will be the fruit of the Spirit at work within us. The key quality is self-control which leads to a gentle humility, and integrity or faithfulness. The opposite of self-control in this context is to be a control freak. Control freaks need to be in control of every situation, and seek to control every relationship they are involved in. Such driving needs can again be traced back to a totally inadequate view of who you are in Christ. The need to always be in control of every situation is often linked to the experience of never feeling trusted by anyone, and never being able to trust anyone. Now you have an unbreakable foundation of trust. As you walk with God you will learn to trust God completely, discover His word to be utterly reliable, and His Spirit constantly with you and caring for you.

This is the work of the Holy Spirit within us. He assures us constantly of who we are in Christ. "Having believed, you were marked in him with a seal, the promised Holy Spirit, who is a deposit guaranteeing our inheritance until the redemption of those who are God's possession – to the praise of his glory" (Ephesians 1:13–14). We, the redeemed, are on a lifelong journey, led and empowered by the Holy Spirit as we respond to all that He is doing in us. And so we move towards that destination of Christlikeness. One day we will arrive: "But we know that when he appears, we shall be like him, for we shall see him as he is" (1 John 3:2).

CHAPTER TWELVE

Parakaleo

We have a battle on our hands, both to get and to keep the right foundation for our identity. So much in our culture can be used to attack our self-worth, leading to the wrong basis for our identity. The British seem to have a particular gift for undermining people; the cutting put-down and the clever comeback are celebrated. When someone enjoys success, it seems many feel their immediate mission is to ensure that success doesn't go to that person's head. "Don't get too big for your boots" and "Pride comes before a fall" are two sayings that show this mission has been around for a while. And it's not just the British. In Australia, particularly, you will hear of the "tall poppy syndrome" – the belief that highly successful people need to be cut down to size.

Building up or tearing down?

We are called to be different; to build others up, not to put them down. We are to "do nothing out of selfish ambition or vain conceit, but in humility consider others better than yourselves" (Philippians 2:3). Paul continues, "Each of you should look not only to your own interests, but also to the interests of others" (verse 4). Our supreme example in this is the Lord Jesus, who was willing to "make himself nothing" (verse 7) so that we, who were nothing, might be something. He was ready to be made sin that we might be made righteous. God the Father was willing for His perfect Son "to be sin for us, so that in him we might become the righteousness of God" (2 Corinthians 5:21).

Read John 3:22–30.

One way in which the Holy Spirit transforms us is by taking away the constant drive to promote ourselves. There will now even be a willingness to promote others at the apparent expense of ourselves. The disciples of John the Baptist had no doubt made considerable sacrifices. He certainly wasn't popular in all circles, and his disciples were probably caught up in the opposition. But it was really all going quite well. Numbers were growing, "people were constantly coming to be baptized" (John 3:23). But then a problem arose. The popularity of another preacher was growing. "It is that man you spoke to us about, Jesus from Nazareth," said John's disciples. "Everyone is going to him" (verse 26). "We are losing out here," they may have said. "Our status is being diminished, and we have made sacrifices to get where we are." John's response is beautiful: "A man can receive only what is given him from heaven" (verse 27). In other words, it is a sovereign God who places His servants in positions and gives them the tasks that they are to do. John knows his role is to be the forerunner for the Messiah and is clearly perfectly content in that calling. "'You yourselves can testify that I said, 'I am not the Christ but am sent ahead of him'" (verse 28). His disciples are concerned by the emergence of Jesus, but John rejoices. "The bride belongs to the bridegroom. The friend who attends the bridegroom waits and listens for him, and is full of joy when he hears the bridegroom's voice" (verse 29).

What a terrific principle in Christian ministry. It is not my job to make a name for myself. I want to sink into the background wherever possible, so that He has the pre-eminence. Calvin wrote, "Those who win the church over to themselves rather than to Christ faithlessly violate the marriage which they ought to honour".[18] John then gives us a great principle of the Christian life and of Christian ministry: "He must become greater; I must become less" (verse 30). John seems to be deliberately giving away his disciples. As Leon Morris writes, "It is not particularly easy in this world to gather followers about one for a serious purpose. But when they are gathered it is infinitely harder to detach them, and firmly insist that they go after another. It is the measure of John's greatness that he did just that."[19]

---

18 Quoted in Leon Morris, *New International Commentary on the New Testament*, Grand Rapids, MI: Eerdmans, 1971.

19 Leon Morris, *New International Commentary on the New Testament*, Grand Rapids, MI: Eerdmans, 1971, page 242.

The oxygen of encouragement

Saul's conversion caused quite a stir. The persecutor now faced persecution. The Damascus believers had to help this remarkable convert out of the city for his own safety and theirs. He headed for Jerusalem and there "he tried to join the disciples, but they were all afraid of him, not believing that he really was a disciple" (Acts 9:26).

It's difficult to imagine how Saul must have been feeling. His whole world view had just been turned on its head. Imagine his confusion as, prostrate on the ground, he asked, "Who are you, Lord?" (Acts 9:5). No doubt he was still trying to get his head around everything that had happened in the last few hours. His colleagues of a few days ago would probably now be his persecutors, unless they were simply waiting for him to come to his senses. Those who should have been his friends couldn't believe that what he said had happened to him could possibly be true. "We know God saves," they may have commented, "but does he save people like Saul? With his history?"

Where would it all have ended without Barnabas? "But Barnabas took him and brought him to the apostles" (Acts 9:27). Saul's predicament is a summons to the sensitive son of encouragement to get alongside and help him. But there is no let up. Saul soon hit trouble in Jerusalem. After a period of freedom and witness (verse 28), the Grecian Jews tried to kill him (verse 29). "What shall we do with him now? He's becoming a bit too hot to handle." Maybe sending him back to his home town was the safest option (verse 30).

Eight years pass and we don't hear much about Saul. He may have been evangelizing in Syria and Cilicia (Galatians 1:21). Did he begin to suffer the hardship mentioned in 2 Corinthians 11:23–27 during this time? Was he disinherited by his family? They were clearly zealous Jews (Philippians 3:5). It was probably a really tough period, maybe containing physical beatings, possible family isolation, and not too many other believers in Tarsus.

"Then Barnabas went to Tarsus to look for Saul, and when he found him, he brought him to Antioch. So for a whole year Barnabas and Saul met with the church and taught great numbers of people" (Acts 11:25–26). It was a brilliant year of laying a ministry foundation on which Paul would build for the years to come. When you think of Paul's contribution to the church, aren't you grateful to Barnabas?

We saw in chapter ten that one of the Greek words used to describe the Holy Spirit is *Paraclete*, the one who comes alongside to help us. We are now called to get alongside brothers and sisters who need our encouragement. Those who had come to Christ through Paul's ministry in Thessalonica had done so "in spite of severe suffering" (1 Thessalonians 1:6). Paul then had to leave them in a big hurry as he was in danger of losing his life at the hands of an unruly mob. He was desperate for news of how they were doing. But the only word coming from the church was that Paul had become the focus of criticism there. Paul decided to send Timothy, "who is our brother and God's fellow worker in spreading the gospel of Christ, to strengthen and encourage you in your faith" (1 Thessalonians 3:2). The word translated "encourage" is the Greek word *parakaleo*, which means "I call to my side, call for, or summons". Paul was convinced that the Thessalonian believers must have been suffering. This was a call to action for him. They needed someone alongside them to help, and he couldn't go. So he sent Timothy. The struggles, the problems, of our brothers and sisters call out to us. They summon us to get alongside and offer help and encouragement.

Sometimes you don't need to speak in order to build up your struggling brother or sister. Just being there with someone when they are struggling, putting an arm around them, can be all that is needed. As we have seen, Job's friends might have been truer friends if they had kept their mouths shut and simply been there for him. I just took a few minutes off from writing to go and have a chat with my wife, Win. We thought back over two particularly tough periods in Christian ministry when we had really been in need of encouragement. Many of the encouragements that came to us as we thought of those days were acts of kindness. There was the cheque sent by a friend so that we could go away for the weekend and "just get away from it all". A rota was arranged through a particularly difficult week so that we didn't need to make an evening meal each day.

Soon after this conversation with Win, a friend who had worked with me in Operation Mobilisation for many years paid a visit. I asked him about encouragement in hard times. Immediately he told me of the toughest period of all. In the middle of it, a friend had come alongside to help. Seeing how much he was struggling, he offered him two weeks at his cottage in Yorkshire. It was a very special time. Each day he would read, listen to a tape, and then go for a hike. Interestingly he came home from that time convinced of many things he should no longer be doing. He realized he had been trying to live up to the expectations he thought others had of him. Now he was content just to be what God had made him to be and to do what he felt God wanted of him. It had been a crash course in identity!

These acts of mercy and kindness are brilliant and sometimes all that is needed, but an appropriate word of encouragement at an appropriate moment can also make a huge difference. What a powerful weapon the tongue is, both to tear down and to build up.

A weapon of mass...

We can speak words of encouragement and life to one another, or words of destruction and death. The rabbis at the time of Christ taught (paraphrased from William Barclay):

"Life and death are in the hand of the tongue. Has the tongue a hand? No! But as the hand kills, so does the tongue. But there is a difference. The hand kills only at close quarters. The tongue is called an arrow because it can kill at a distance. But I say more. An arrow can kill at forty or fifty paces, but of the tongue it is said in the seventy-third Psalm, 'Their mouths lay claim to heaven and their tongues take possession of the earth.' And that indeed is the peril of the uncontrolled tongue. A man can ward off a blow with the hand because the striker is at close quarters, but you can drop a malicious word or repeat a scandalous story and a man can be devastated thousands of miles away. So the tongue is much more powerful than an arrow or a fist."

When David is fleeing for his life from Saul just after learning that Saul "had come out to take his life" (1 Samuel 23:15), "Jonathan went to David at Horesh and helped him to find strength in God" (verse 16). This was an act of great courage by Jonathan, and put his life in jeopardy, but it was an act of true friendship. I am sure the presence of Jonathan must have been a huge encouragement. It is a scene of dreadful betrayal. David and his men had just rescued the people of Keilah from the Philistines, only to hear from God that they would now hand him over to Saul (1 Samuel 23:1–12). Immediately after Jonathan's visit, the Ziphites, in whose area David was now hiding from Saul, were intending to hand him over to the king (verse 19). How timely this visit of a faithful friend was for David. But there was not only the encouragement of Jonathan's presence, he brought the encouragement of God's purpose. "'Don't be afraid,' he said. 'My father Saul will not lay a hand on you. You shall be king over Israel, and I will be second to you. Even my father Saul knows this'" (verse 17). It is a choice word of encouragement, just what David needed to hear at exactly the time he needed to hear it.

So are we going to be those who use our lips to build up or to tear down? Meditate on these verses from Proverbs for a few moments:

"The soothing tongue is a tree of life, but a perverse tongue crushes the spirit" (Proverbs 15:4).

"Gracious words are a honeycomb, sweet to the soul and healing to the bones" (Proverbs 16:24).

"The lips of the righteous nourish many" (Proverbs 10:21).

"The words of the reckless pierce like swords, but the tongue of the wise brings healing" (Proverbs 12:18).

"A perverse person stirs up dissension, and a gossip separates close friends" (Proverbs 16:28).

"Whoever would foster love covers over an offence, but whoever repeats the matter separates close friends" (Proverbs 17:9).

"To answer before listening – that is folly and shame" (Proverbs 18:13).

"A gentle answer turns away wrath, but a harsh word stirs up anger" (Proverbs 15:1).

So many struggle with self-worth and identity issues, and so many can help with a choice word at an appropriate moment.

This is what the Christian church should be – a body of encouraged encouragers. Those who know who they are in Christ should be going out of their way to see their brothers and sisters established and firm in their own identity in Christ.

The picture Paul paints of the body of Christ is a beautiful image of mutual support and encouragement. Every member in the body is needed. Each has a unique and essential part to play (1 Corinthians 12:15–20). The parts of the body are intended to have an equal concern for each other. When one part is honoured, there is a celebration attended by all (verses 25–26). It is a beautiful picture, of a place where you can relax and be all that God made you to be, where your strengths and victories will be celebrated and shared, and your weaknesses and failures will be seen and heard as calls to come alongside and help you. Sadly that is not always how the body of Christ is, but that is how it should be. More than ever in today's culture it is what the body of Christ must become.

CHAPTER THIRTEEN

Identity and Leadership

Read Matthew 20:20–28:

Then the mother of Zebedee's sons came to Jesus with her sons and, kneeling down, asked a favour of him.

"What is it you want?" he asked.

She said, "Grant that one of these two sons of mine may sit at your right and the other at your left in your kingdom."

"You don't know what you are asking," Jesus said to them. "Can you drink the cup I am going to drink?"

"We can," they answered.

Jesus said to them, "You will indeed drink from my cup, but to sit at my right or left is not for me to grant. These places belong to those for whom they have been prepared by my Father."

When the ten heard about this, they were indignant with the two brothers. Jesus called them together and said, "You know that the rulers of the

> *Gentiles lord it over them, and their high officials exercise authority over them. Not so with you. Instead, whoever wants to become great among you must be your servant, and whoever wants to be first must be your slave – just as the Son of Man did not come to be served, but to serve, and to give his life as a ransom for many."*

Thank God for the gift of leadership. Where would we be without it? Thank God for the men of Issachar who "understood the times and knew what Israel should do" (1 Chronicles 12:32), and the women too. This is the age of independence when everyone wants to do their own thing, and believes they should be free to do so. There is a real danger that in the church, we will bow to the spirit of the age, and become a leaderless people. God gives the calling and the gift of leadership to some of His children. He intends that churches and Christian organizations should be led by those to whom He has given these gifts. He does not intend that these people should just be facilitators: they should be true leaders.

The leadership calling – to build up others

This calling of leadership, however, is given for a very specific purpose. God gives this gift for the same reason that "he gave some to be apostles, some to be prophets, some to be evangelists, and some to be pastors and teachers". The purpose is "to prepare God's people for works of service, so that the body of Christ may be built up" (Ephesians 4:11–12). These callings and gifts are given to the body, and they are for the good of the body of Christ. In Colossians 1:28 Paul presents the goal of his ministry, and his twofold goal should surely be the passion of every Christian leader. It is to "proclaim him" and to "present everyone perfect (fully mature) in Christ". Tragically there are some leaders who, often without realizing it, "present everyone dependent on them". All the energy in the church or organization flows from the bottom up to bolster and support them, with very little good cascading down the other way. In Romans 12:4–8 Paul makes very clear what God intended when He gave the gift of leadership to some within His church:

> *Just as each one of us has one body with many members, and these members do not all have the same function, so in Christ we who are many form one body, and each member belongs to all the others. We all have different gifts, according to the grace given us. If a man's gift is prophesying, let him use it in proportion to his faith. If it is serving, let him serve; if it is teaching, let him teach; if it is encouraging, let him encourage; if it is contributing to the needs of others, let him give generously; if it is leadership, let him govern diligently; if it is showing mercy, let him do it cheerfully.*

Threatened leaders destroy

In more than forty years of leadership experience, I have noticed one problem more than any other which destroys good leadership. This problem also makes many sincere leaders themselves become destroyers. It is the problem of threatened leaders. These leaders are insecure people. They are the kind of people who always feel the need to prove themselves. They tend to be competitive and restless. The leadership role and title that they acquire becomes the basis of their security. It becomes their identity. "I am the director of..." The thought of this position ever being taken from them therefore threatens their whole identity. They will defend their position at all costs. Anyone whom they see, or others identify, as having the gifts to one day replace them is in danger. Some leaders make careful and deliberate plans to remove or destroy any potential competitor.

In my time in leadership I have met very few leaders who deliberately plan to be abusive. Insecure leaders can move on to being abusive or "toxic" in their leadership without realising it. I have had to challenge a number of leaders about abusive behaviour; and invariably they have been totally shocked. They have been amazed and often deeply upset that anyone should describe them this way. In many cases it has not been long before total denial and absolute defensiveness have set in. Added to this genuine inability to see these traits within themselves is another major problem. Their weaknesses are also their strengths. They appear to be loving, caring people with engaging personalities. They are almost always extremely hard-working and apparently loyal to anyone above them. Those abused therefore often remain silent, realizing how difficult it is going to be to convince anyone of the problem.

When people eventually do speak out, they often suffer further abuse as no one else sees the problem; the insecure leader seems so good that those voicing concerns are condemned as troublemakers. When the German Sixth Army had been surrounded in Stalingrad by the Russian forces, the opportunity to break out of the stranglehold decreased as time passed. Hitler and the German hierarchy insisted they could supply the surrounded forces by an air bridge, and if they held on, a rescue force would deliver them. Most of those on the ground knew this was a pipe dream. Many things made it impossible, not the least the weather. But Antony Beevor writes, "Apart from Richthofen, however, Luftwaffe officers, either within the 'Kessel'[20] or outside did not dare speak out. 'It was defeatism if you voiced doubts,' said one of them."[21] This silence cost thousands of lives.

What does the Bible say about authority in leadership? What kind of authority is it? Where does it come from? What is it to be used for? When and how is that authority abused?

In writing of the problem of abusive leadership, the last thing that I want to do is to discourage leaders from truly leading. It is clear from Scripture that God invests leaders with authority. This authority is given by God so that leaders can lead. Is it not the case that in so many homes, churches,

20 This refers to the "pocket" in which most of the German troops were trapped.

21 Anthony Beevor, *Stalingrad*, Harmondsworth: Penguin, 1999, page 280.

and Christian organizations we are suffering from an absence of leadership – an absence of those who have sought God and have a vision from Him which, if wisely implemented, will make a real and positive difference in the progress of the kingdom? God gives these leaders real authority to implement this vision.

Ephesus was a very strategic city, the principal city of Asia Minor. During his more than two years of ministry there, Paul had witnessed a truly remarkable work of God. From Ephesus, the gospel spread to all of Asia Minor and churches were planted throughout the province. The significance of this city, both politically and as the centre of this work of God, meant that it was vital that Paul had the right person as the leader of the church there. Paul's choice is Timothy, but he considered himself too young for such a strategic role; he was naturally timid and probably reluctant to move into such a position. One of the reasons Paul writes the letter to him, which we know today as First Timothy, is to encourage him in the job and to encourage the church to recognize the authority that came with it.

Paul immediately uses the language of authority. He urges Timothy to stay at Ephesus, "so that you may command certain men not to teach false doctrines any longer nor to devote themselves to myths and endless genealogies" (1 Timothy 1:3–4). The word translated as "command" would, among other uses at the time, be the kind of word used in a military setting to mean "to give strict orders". In 1 Timothy 4:11, Paul uses the same word again: "Command and teach these things." He urges Titus also to use his authority in silencing false teachers. "Rebuke them sharply, so that they will be sound in the faith" (Titus 1:13). "They must be silenced" (Titus 1:11). The context of these statements is dealing with opposition and false teaching, but there are more general statements underlining the authority God gives to leaders in, for example, Hebrews 13:7–17.

Paul was also not slow in writing of his own authority. In 2 Corinthians 10, he is preparing the church for a visit he is planning to make to them. Opposition there to him has been brutal and longstanding. Paul is preparing for what could be described as a showdown on his third visit. He writes, "We demolish arguments and every pretension that sets itself up against the knowledge of God, and we take captive every thought to make it obedient to Christ. And we will be ready to punish every act of disobedience, once your obedience is complete" (verses 5–6).

Paul's authority was, of course, apostolic authority, but we see in this passage in 2 Corinthians that even this authority he wants to use with great care. Though he is planning strong actions when he gets to Corinth, he would much prefer not to have to throw his weight around. He appeals to them by "the meekness and gentleness of Christ" (verse 1). He "begs" them (verse 2). Paul knows that even this apostolic authority must only be used to build up the church. When it is exercised for any other purpose then he urges believers to resist it (Galatians 1:8).

Under or over

If you are in leadership, you need to ask whether you are seeking to get people under your authority so that you can rule them, or seeking to get under people so that you can support them, serve them, and build them up. In 2 Corinthians 13, Paul returns to the issue of authority and how it is to be used. This third visit to Corinth will become a "showdown" visit if they do not take certain steps. He is writing to them in advance of the visit, hoping that if they get their act together, he will "not have to be harsh in my use of authority" (verse 10).

Then he states the nature and the purpose of this authority. It is a God-given authority – the Lord gave it to him, and the purpose is "for building you up, not for tearing you down". It is important to recognize again that Paul is referring to his apostolic authority, but this is surely the purpose of all God-given authority in Christian leadership. Divine authority is not given to build leaders up but those they are leading, and it is certainly not given to tear down those we are called to lead. So Paul is not concerned here about his own reputation as a leader. He is content if they "do what is right even though we may seem to have failed" (verse 7). He is "glad whenever we are weak but you are strong" (verse 9). "Everything we do," he writes in 12:19, "is for your strengthening."

Insecure leaders, however, have a constant need to build themselves up to bolster their own feelings of insecurity and vulnerability. They are people who tragically have failed to find their security in their relationship with Christ and so have to look elsewhere. They often rely upon a position for this sense of security and worth. The less secure a leader, the more important title and position will be to them. Jesus warned us of the dangers of this. "But you are not to be called 'Rabbi', for you have only one Master and you are all brothers. And do not call anyone on earth 'father', for you have one Father, and he is in heaven. Nor are you to be called 'teacher', for you have one Teacher, the Christ. The greatest among you will be your servant. For whoever exalts himself will be humbled, and whoever humbles himself will be exalted" (Matthew 23:8–12). Jesus is here clearly condemning the yearning after rank and position.

This yearning is not normally evident when a person is appointed to leadership – if it were, maybe potentially abusive leaders could be weeded out a lot earlier.

Leadership is often stressful as well as joyful. In the stress, old weaknesses and characteristics people were not even aware of in themselves can come to the fore. If the leader's identity is not firmly rooted in being a child of God these characteristics begin to take prominence. It can be very gradual and one day people realize the person now leading them seems very different from the person they appointed.

I am the director of...

Once the insecure leader has a title and position, they will do almost anything to retain it. This position and title become their identity. They cannot imagine life without these things. They possess a huge drive in order to protect their position. Their performance in the job becomes the focus of their lives. Initially, of course, this can be very attractive to those who have put them in the position and those who work with them. It is often equated with true Christian commitment, the willingness for sacrifice. Maintaining the image then becomes essential. It becomes more important to look spiritual than to be spiritual, to look in control than to be in control, to seem to have a wonderful marriage than to actually have one, to appear to be deeply appreciated by your colleagues than to actually be appreciated. There is real tragedy here. When we constantly have to cover over the reality, we are not going to go for help for what is really going on in our lives. There is the inexhaustible store of the grace of God available to us, but we are not going to go near because we cannot afford to admit the problem, often even to ourselves, and certainly not to anyone else. To do that might bring down the whole house of cards.

If image is everything, then you will be constantly waiting and listening for the affirmation of others. We all appreciate praise, but for the insecure leader this becomes an almost overwhelming need. Any criticism immediately becomes a major crisis. It is an attack against the image and, if not dealt with, the house of cards might wobble. People are viewed by the leader as either supportive of them or suspect and dangerous. Sadly it can be the case that people are loved by the leader until they raise questions. The change from being loved to being considered dangerous takes place in a moment. You can find yourself moved from the leader's support group to being a *persona non grata* at the drop of a hat. And this is because, in questioning, you have attacked their identity – without in any way meaning to do so.

It is not long in these situations before a secretive culture dominates. The leader has to hide what is real; failing to do so will destroy the image by ruining the performance. The followers also begin to turn in on themselves, keeping their thoughts strictly to themselves or within the group who have felt the leader's wrath. In many groups where there is abusive leadership, there develops what David Johnson[22] refers to as the "can't talk rule". "If you speak about the problem you become the problem." "We didn't have all these problems in the group until you started shooting your mouth off."

This culture of secretiveness is often given divine justification: "We need to protect the testimony from those who will never understand us." The counsel given to those who break the secretive culture and speak out is also often expressed in highly "spiritual" terms. "You were clearly angry at the time; you did not 'speak the truth in love'." Another favourite is, "You have a critical spirit." Unless the person is very secure in their own walk with God, such counsel leaves them struggling with guilt and drives them back even deeper into the secretive culture.

The Bible is, of course, often used to bolster the leader's authority. If their knowledge of the Bible is greater than yours then that knowledge can become power and can be used in an abusive way. The Scriptures which are meant

---

22 *The Subtle Power of Spiritual Abuse*, David Johnson & Jeff Van Vonderen (Bethany House), page 68.

to pierce our own hearts can be used as a weapon to drive others. A common example of abuse is where disloyalty to or disagreement with the leadership is equated with disloyalty to God. You will often find that those who leave the church or the organization are described as disloyal or unspiritual as a result. Or indeed they are told that they are going to hell, and that any member of their family who leaves with them has the same destination.

Recognizing abusive leadership

When we recognize some of the basic principles of good leadership, abusive leadership may be easier to recognize. Are the fruits of the Spirit evident in the life and leadership of the leader? No one is perfect, everyone will fail, but would you describe the leader as normally loving, joyful, peaceful, patient, kind, good, displaying faithfulness (true to their word, for example) gentle, and self-controlled?

Where a leader is leading with the authority given by God there will be a desire to lead in a way which honours God who has given the authority, and therefore you would expect to see the characteristics which would honour God in that leader's life.

Secondly, if the leader's authority is from God then there will be a commitment to Scripture as God's authoritative word. It is interesting that as Paul seeks to help Timothy establish his authority, he counsels him to "be diligent to present yourself approved to God as a workman who does not need to be ashamed, accurately handling the word of truth" (2 Timothy 2:15, NASB). Your authority will be seen as you handle the word accurately, because your authority is from God and this is His authoritative word.

Thirdly, is the leader concerned to see the development of those they are leading? True leaders have sufficient security in themselves and in their relationship with Christ that they don't have to compete with anyone else. When someone else succeeds they rejoice and support that person so that they are able to do even better. They will not take credit which belongs to someone else. Equally, when they do well themselves they will not hide from recognition. The person who constantly seems to back away from recognition may be displaying genuine humility but it is possible they may be looking for more praise for their accomplishments, in order to bolster their lack of self-worth.

Fourthly, is there space for open discussion and disagreement? All matters should be open for discussion in a healthy group. On some points there may be disagreement, but that disagreement should not lead to disruption of relationship and fellowship. In a healthy group there should be the freedom to agree to disagree, to suspend discussion on certain issues if they are causing excessive tension and return to them later.

Fifthly, is there accountability? Without clear accountability for the leader there is always enormous potential for corruption of all kinds. Does the organization have an active board of directors? In the local church is there a rigorous board of elders, who hold the leader accountable? If it is a leadership team do they hold one another accountable?

Are these relationships truly meaningful? Did the leader of the organization choose his own board? Have they chosen friends who may be too close to hold them truly accountable?

And what if you now see yourself as an insecure leader who may even have slipped without realizing it before into being an abusive leader? Don't minimize the problem. The traits which lead to this are often deeply ingrained. It may well be necessary to stand down from your leadership position at least for a time and work on the areas of insecurity in your life. But all is not lost, and God is the God of redemption. Many of the characteristics seen in insecure leaders are vital. Your drive, your desire to achieve, your commitment are all great leadership characteristics. If the insecurities can be dealt with and your leadership can by God's grace be for the right motive, then, with the right safeguards, you could be a very effective leader. Those safeguards would include realistic accountability relationships with people who know the problems there have been in your leadership. There must be a commitment to work, probably with your accountability partners, to see a greater balance in your life. Up until this point your work has probably been far too dominant in your life. You need to give much more time to relationships, including your relationship with the Lord. The focus of that relationship up until this point has probably been that of a servant. You need to give time to foster your relationship as a son or daughter. And by the way, there is nothing wrong with having a good hobby, or even two!

Conclusion

I began my work as an itinerant preacher when I was quite young. Too young, I think, looking back. I soon became well known, at least in the Christian circles I frequented at the time. Some placed me on a pedestal, and I am afraid I loved it! The more invitations that came, and the larger the meetings I was addressing, the more fulfilled I felt. I was being helped to find my identity, my self-worth, in what I was doing, and in the apparent success I was achieving. But I really didn't need help. Finding my identity there seemed to come naturally, without effort. You can see whom I was doing Christian work for? Me!

Over the decades, as position and titles, some of which I mentioned at the beginning of this book, have been given to me, the danger of making these the basis of my worth has never been far away. How subtle my enemy is. How insidious the temptation to make my service for Christ a self-serving exercise. After all these years, it is still a regular necessity to remind myself of the true basis of my worth.

I am made in the image of my Creator.

I have been redeemed by the shed blood of His Son.

I have been adopted into God's family and can call God "Abba".

The verses in Galatians 4:6–7 are as important as ever for me. "Because you are sons, God sent the Spirit of his Son into our hearts, the Spirit who calls out, '*Abba*, Father.' So you are no longer a slave, but a son; and since you are a son, God has made you also an heir."

After his remarkable conversion, John Newton, the former slave trader, wanted to always remember all that God had done for him. He wanted to remember the depths he had plumbed and the heights God had now raised him to. He wrote in large letters the words of Deuteronomy 15:15 and placed them above his mantelpiece: "Thou shalt remember that thou wast a bondman [or slave] in the land of Egypt, and the Lord thy God redeemed thee" (KJV).

Should we make a modern translation of that our screen saver?

After Justin Welby discovered that the man he had thought was his father was not, he made a moving statement which included words which I think sum up what I have been trying to say in this book.

"I know that I find who I am in Jesus Christ, not in genetics, and my identity in him never changes. At the very outset of my inauguration service three years ago, Evangeline Kanagasooriam, a young member of the Canterbury cathedral congregation, said: 'We greet you in the name of Christ. Who are you, and why do you request entry?' To which I responded: 'I am Justin, a servant of Jesus Christ, and I come as one seeking the grace of God to travel with you in his service together.' What has changed? Nothing."

That's it! Identity secure in Christ, a foundation no storm can destroy.

"So, what do you think? With God on our side like this, how can we lose? If God didn't hesitate to put everything on the line for us, embracing our condition and exposing himself to the worst by sending his own Son, is there anything else he wouldn't gladly and freely do for us? And who would dare tangle with God by messing with one of God's chosen? Who would dare even to point a finger? The One who died for us – who was raised to life for us! – is in the presence of God at this very moment sticking up for us. Do you think anyone is going to be able to drive a wedge between us and Christ's love for us? There is no way! Not trouble, not hard times, not hatred, nor hunger, not homelessness, not bullying threats, not backstabbing, not even the worst sins listed in Scripture:

"They kill us in cold blood because they hate you. We're sitting ducks; they pick us off one by one. None of this fazes us because Jesus loves us. I'm absolutely convinced that nothing – nothing living or dead, angelic or demonic, today or tomorrow, high or low, thinkable or unthinkable – absolutely *nothing* can get between us and God's love because of the way that Jesus our Master has embraced us" (Romans 8:31–39, *The Message*).